# *Schultz's Best*
# BIG NOTE PIANO
# ENCYCLOPEDIA

## 2nd Edition

## Popular Piano Arrangements
## by Robert Schultz

© 2000 WARNER BROS. PUBLICATIONS
All Rights Reserved Including Public Performance for Profit

Editor: Robert Schultz
Project Manager: Tony Esposito
Production Coordinator: Hank Fields
Book Design: Odalis Soto

# CONTENTS

## POPULAR HITS

## MOVIE & TV MUSIC

## POP & ROCK CLASSICS

## AMERICAN & FOLK SONGS

## ALL-TIME FAVORITES

## CLASSICAL THEMES

*From the Original Motion Picture Soundtrack "THE THREE MUSKETEERS"*

# ALL FOR LOVE

Written by
BRYAN ADAMS, ROBERT JOHN "MUTT" LANGE
and MICHAEL KAMEN
*Arranged by ROBERT SCHULTZ*

**Moderately slow** ♩ = 76

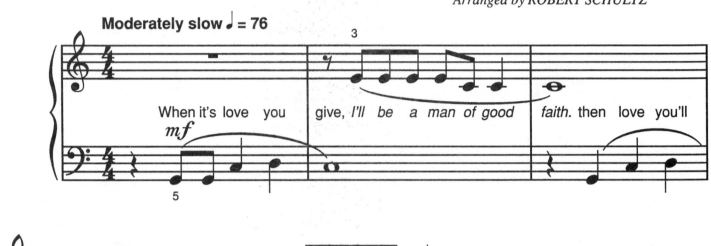

When it's love you give, *I'll be a man of good faith.* then love you'll

live. *I'll make a stand I won't blink.* I'll be the rock you can build on,

be there when you're old, to have and to hold. 2.When there's love in-

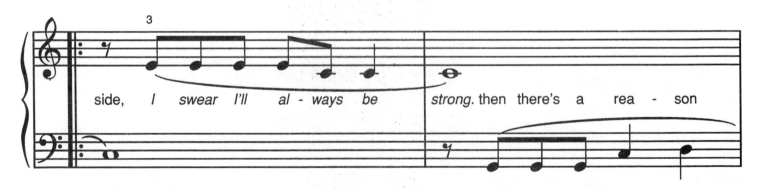

side, *I swear I'll al - ways be strong.* then there's a rea - son

All for Love - 3 - 1

AS006

6

Verse 3:
When it's love you make, *I'll be the fire in your night.*
Then it's love you take. *I will defend, I will fight.*
I'll be there when you need me, when honor's at stake, this vow I will make,
That it's all for one and all for love.
*(To Chorus:)*

*From the Original Motion Picture Soundtrack "BEACHES"*

# THE WIND BENEATH MY WINGS

Words and Music by
LARRY HENLEY and JEFF SILBAR
*Arranged by ROBERT SCHULTZ*

The Wind beneath My Wings - 3 - 1
AS006

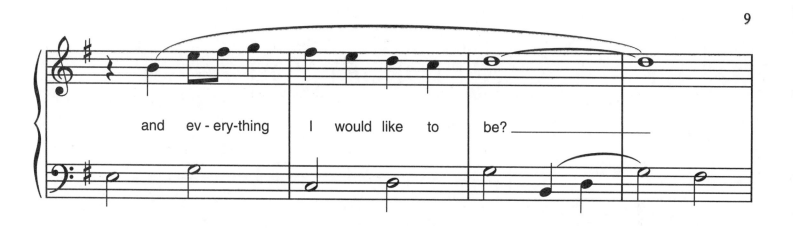

and ev-ery-thing    I   would  like   to    be? _____

I  can fly   high-er  than  an   ea - gle, _____   'cause you are the

*dim.*

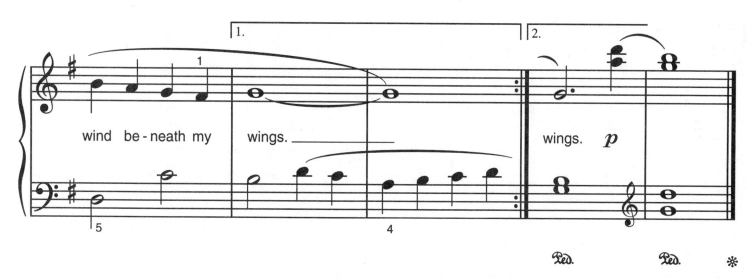

1.

2.

wind be-neath my   wings. _____    wings. *p*

*Ped.*    *Ped.*    *

*Verse 3:*
It might have appeared to go unnoticed,
But I've got it all here in my heart.
I want you to know I know the truth, I know it,
I would be nothing without you.
*(To Chorus:)*

# CAN'T FORGET YOU

Words and Music by
JORGE CASAS, CLAY OSTWALD
and JON SECADA
*Arranged by ROBERT SCHULTZ*

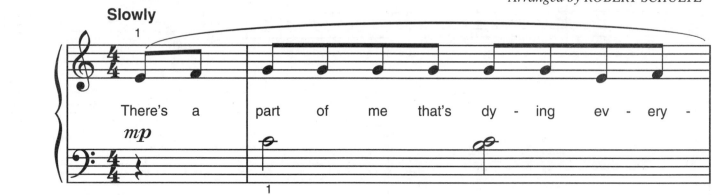

There's a part of me that's dy - ing ev - ery -

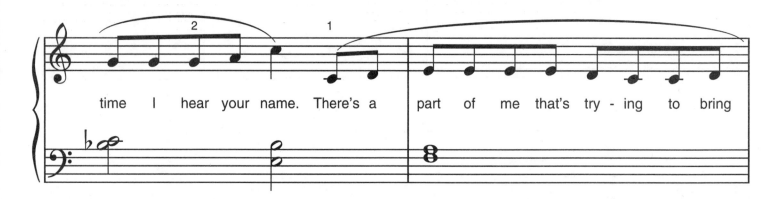

time I hear your name. There's a part of me that's try - ing to bring

back your love a - gain. There are times when I just want to run, but

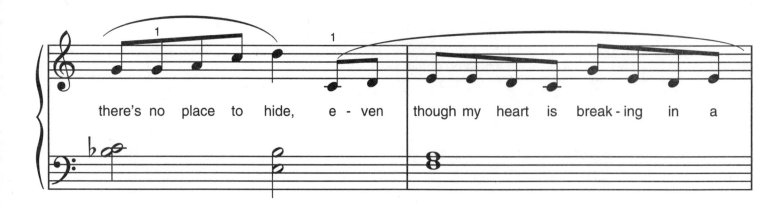

there's no place to hide, e - ven though my heart is break - ing in a

Can't Forget You - 2 - 1
AS006

# FOREVER'S AS FAR AS I'LL GO

Words and Music by
MIKE REID
*Arranged by ROBERT SCHULTZ*

Moderately slow

I'll ad - mit I could feel it the first time that we touched. The

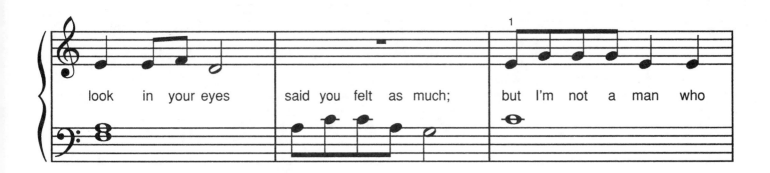

look in your eyes said you felt as much; but I'm not a man who

falls too eas - i - ly. It's best that you know

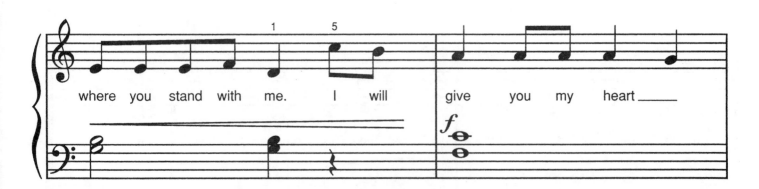

where you stand with me. I will give you my heart

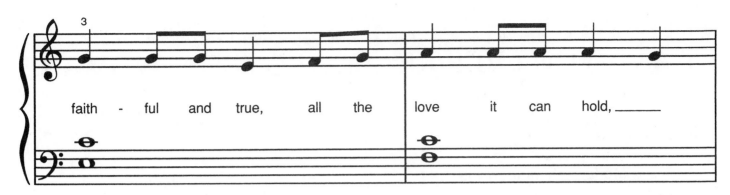

faith - ful and true, all the love it can hold, _____

that's all I can do. I've thought a - bout how

long I'll love you; it's on - ly fair _____ that you

*mf*

know, for - ev - er's as far as I'll go.

*mp*

*p*

Forever's As Far As I'll Go - 2 - 2

*From the Original Motion Picture Soundtrack "DON JUAN DeMARCO"*

# HAVE YOU EVER REALLY LOVED A WOMAN?

Lyrics by
BRYAN ADAMS and
ROBERT JOHN "MUTT" LANGE

Music by
MICHAEL KAMEN
*Arranged by ROBERT SCHULTZ*

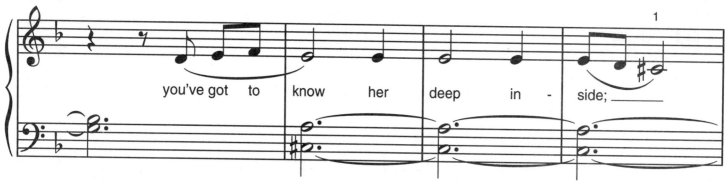

Have You Ever Really Loved a Woman? - 4 - 1
AS006

16

Have You Ever Really Loved a Woman? - 4 - 3

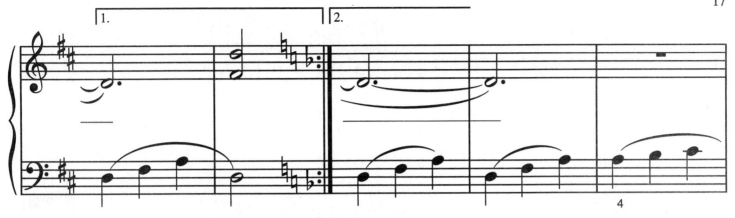

**A little slower**

*p* Tell me, have you ev - er     real - ly,     real - ly, real - ly ev - er

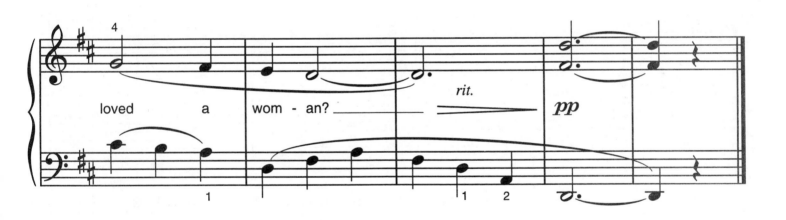

loved     a     wom - an? _____     *rit.* ========     *pp*

*Verse 2:*
To really love a woman, let her hold you, 'til you know how she needs to be touched;
You've got to breathe her, really taster her, 'til you can feel her in your blood.
And when you can see your unborn children in her eyes, you know you really love a woman.
*(To Chorus:)*

*From the Original Soundtrack Album "THE PREACHER'S WIFE"*

# I BELIEVE IN YOU AND ME

Words and Music by
SANDY LINZER and DAVID WOLFERT
*Arranged by ROBERT SCHULTZ*

I Believe in You and Me - 2 - 1
AS006

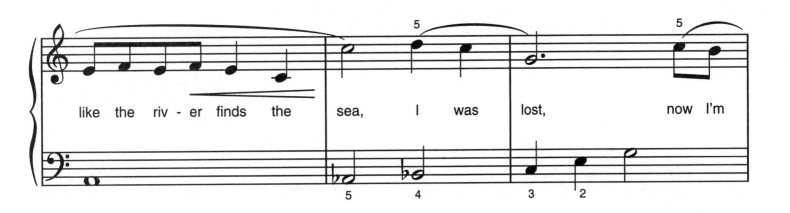

like the riv - er finds the sea, I was lost, now I'm

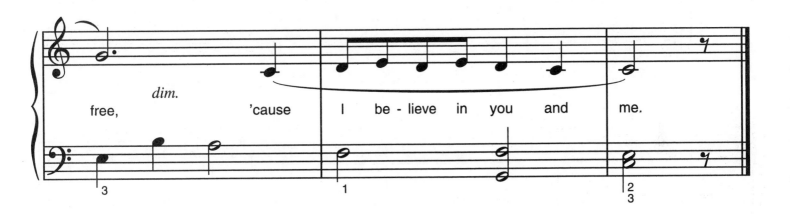

free, *dim.* 'cause I be - lieve in you and me.

*From Touchstone Pictures' "ARMAGEDDON"*

# I DON'T WANT TO MISS A THING

Words and Music by
DIANE WARREN
*Arranged by ROBERT SCHULTZ*

**Moderately**

I Don't Want to Miss a Thing - 2 - 1
AS006

# I STILL BELIEVE IN YOU

Words and Music by
VINCE GILL and JOHN BARLOW JARVIS
*Arranged by ROBERT SCHULTZ*

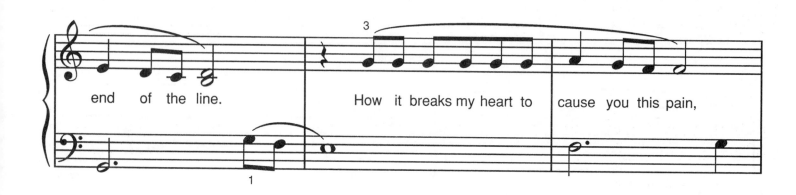

I Still Believe in You - 2 - 1
AS006

**Chorus:**

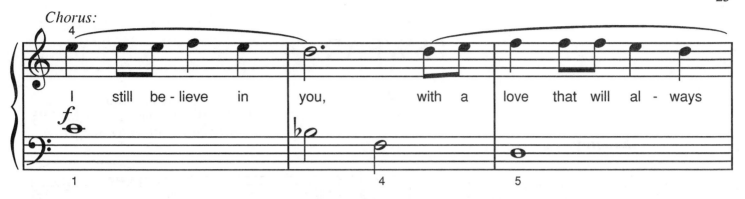

I still be-lieve in you, with a love that will al - ways

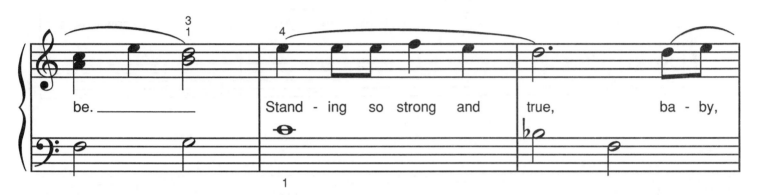

be. Stand - ing so strong and true, ba - by,

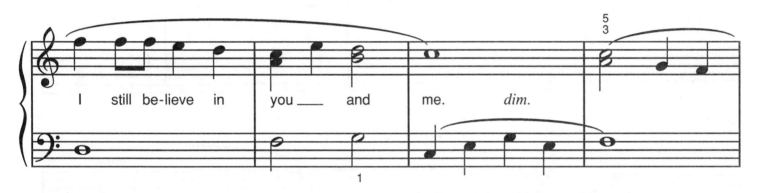

I still be-lieve in you and me. *dim.*

**Verse 2:**
Somewhere along the way, I guess I just lost track,
Only thinking of myself, never looking back.
For all the times I've hurt you, I apologize,
I'm sorry it took so long to finally realize.
Give me the chance to prove
That nothing's worth losing you.
*(To Chorus:)*

# I SWEAR

Words and Music by
GARY BAKER and FRANK MYERS
*Arranged by ROBERT SCHULTZ*

**Moderately slow**

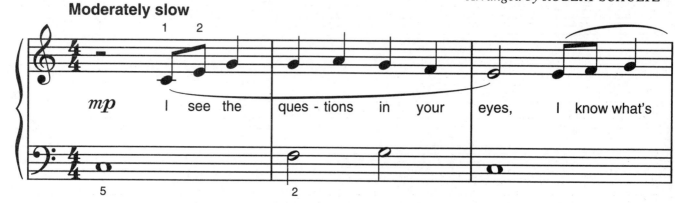

I see the ques-tions in your eyes, I know what's

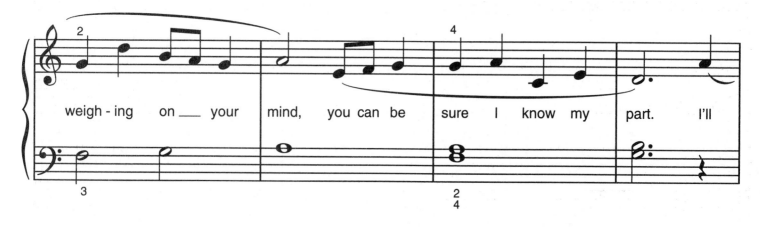

weigh-ing on __ your mind, you can be sure I know my part. I'll

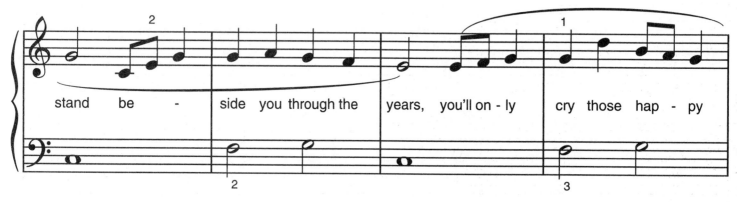

stand be - side you through the years, you'll on - ly cry those hap - py

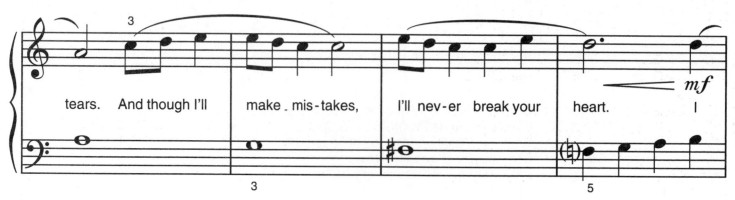

tears. And though I'll make __ mis-takes, I'll nev-er break your heart. I

I Swear - 2 - 1
AS006

# I WILL ALWAYS LOVE YOU

Words and Music by
DOLLY PARTON
*Arranged by ROBERT SCHULTZ*

1. If I should stay, I would on-ly be in your way; so, I'll go, but I know I'll think of you ev-ery step of the way. And I will al-ways love you, will al-ways love you. 2. Bit-ter-sweet mem-o-ries, that is all I'm tak-ing with

Verse 3:
I hope life treats you kind
And I hope you have all you've dreamed of;
And I wish to you joy and happiness,
But above all this I wish you love.
(To Chorus:)

I Will Always Love You - 2 - 2

# IF WE WERE LOVERS

Words and Music by
GLORIA ESTEFAN & EMILIO ESTEFAN, JR.
*Arranged by ROBERT SCHULTZ*

Easily ♩ = 88

*Verse 2:*
If we were lovers, I've waited so long for that day.
I think you feel the same way, you try so hard not to give it away,
Afraid that I'll discover . . .
*(To Bridge:)*

# I'M FREE

Words and Music by
JON SECADA and MIGUEL A. MOREJON
*Arranged by ROBERT SCHULTZ*

**Moderately** ♩ = 100

*I'm Free - 2 - 1*
*AS006*

*Chorus:*

fraid of what I'll find; the sto - ry of our lives, but there's to - mor - row, 'cause I'm

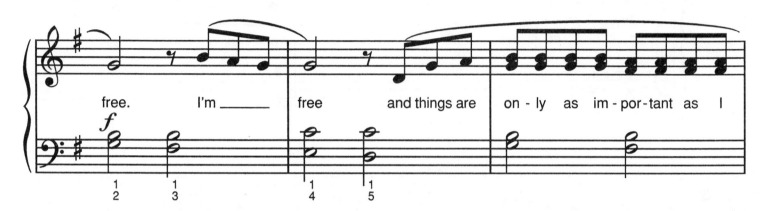

free. I'm _____ free and things are on - ly as im - por - tant as I

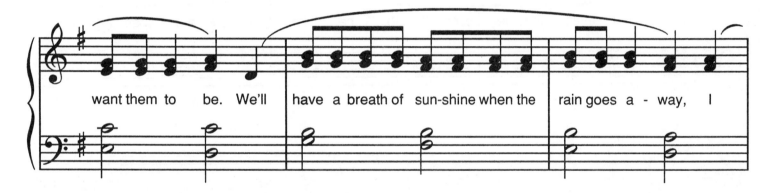

want them to be. We'll have a breath of sun-shine when the rain goes a - way, I

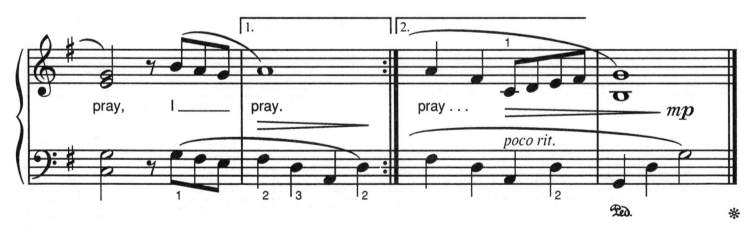

pray, I ___ pray. pray ... *poco rit.* *mp*

*Verse 2:*
Do you need a friend right now on the road that you're going to?
If you get lost, just call me, I'll be there; yes, I'll be right there.
'Cause though I may not have the answers, at least I know what I'm looking for.
Yes, I can do without the sorrow. There's a day after tomorrow, so I'm leaving it behind.
*(To Chorus:)*

I'm Free - 2 - 2

*From Warner Bros. "QUEST FOR CAMELOT"*

# LOOKING THROUGH YOUR EYES

Words and Music by
CAROLE BAYER SAGER
and DAVID FOSTER
*Arranged by ROBERT SCHULTZ*

1. Look at the sky, tell me, what do you see?

Just close your eyes and de - scribe it to me. The heav-ens are spar-kling with

star - light to - night. That's what I see through your eyes.

**Chorus:**

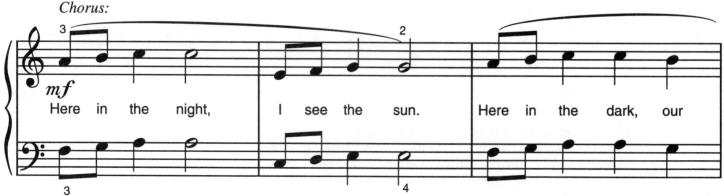

Here in the night, I see the sun. Here in the dark, our

*Looking Through Your Eyes - 2 - 1*
AS006

two hearts are one. It's out of our hands, we can't stop what we have be -

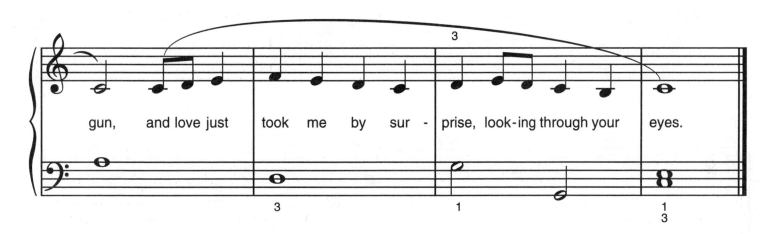

gun, and love just took me by sur - prise, look-ing through your eyes.

*Verse 2:*
I see the heavens each time that you smile.
I hear your heartbeat just go on for miles,
And suddenly I know why life is worthwhile.
That's what I see through your eyes.
*(Chorus:)*

# MORE THAN WORDS

Lyrics and Music by
BETTENCOURT and CHERONE
*Arranged by ROBERT SCHULTZ*

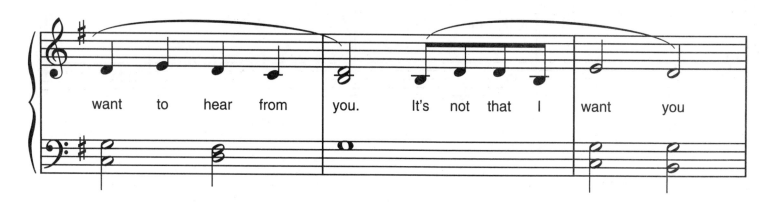

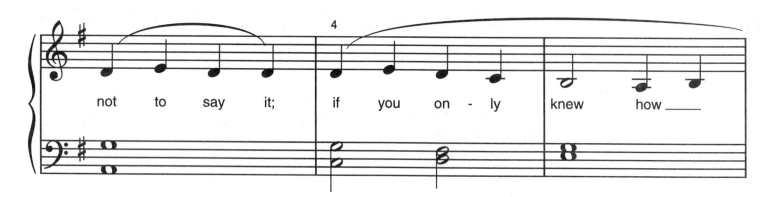

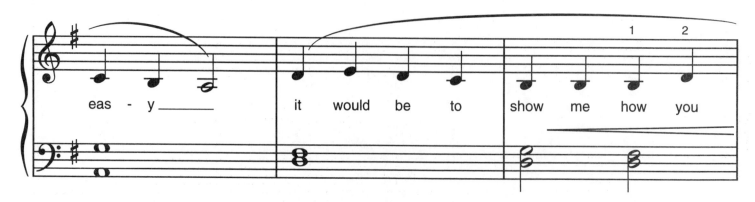

More Than Words - 2 - 1
AS006

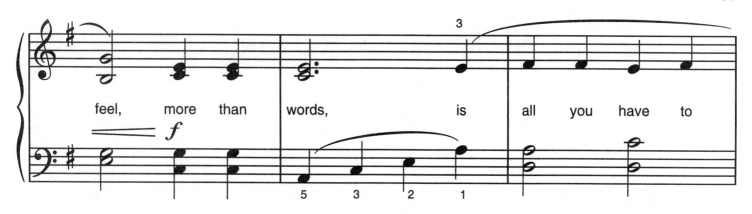

feel,   more than    words,        is    all   you  have to

do   to   make it _____   real.   Then  you   would - n't  have to

say _____    that   you    love  me,  'cause   I'd    al -

read - y       know. _____

More Than Words - 2 - 2

# NOW AND FOREVER

Music and Lyrics by
RICHARD MARX
*Arranged by ROBERT SCHULTZ*

**Coda**

*Verse 2:*
Sometimes I just hold you, too caught up in me to see
I'm holding a fortune that heaven has given to me.
I'll try to show you each and every way I can;
Now and forever, I will be your man.
*(To Bridge:)*


*Verse 3:*
*Solo - 8 bars . . .*
Until the day the ocean doesn't touch the sand;
Now and forever, I will be your man.
*(To Coda)*

# PLEASE FORGIVE ME

Words and Music by BRYAN ADAMS
and ROBERT JOHN "MUTT" LANGE
*Arranged by ROBERT SCHULTZ*

It still feels like our first night to - geth - er.

Feels like the first kiss, it's get - ting bet - ter, ba - by.

No one can bet - ter this, still hold - ing on, you're still the one. ___

First time our eyes met, same feel - ing I get, only feels much strong - er,

Please Forgive Me - 3 - 1
AS006

I'll love you long - er. You still turn the fire ___ on. ___ So, if you're

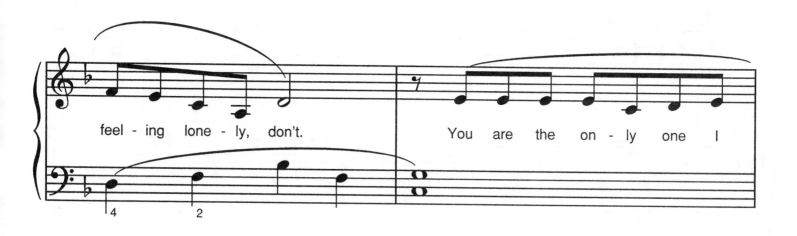

feel - ing lone - ly, don't. You are the on - ly one I

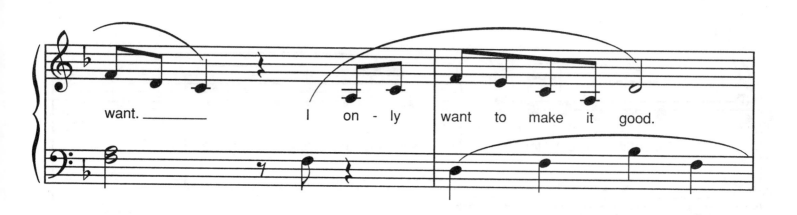

want. _____ I on - ly want to make it good.

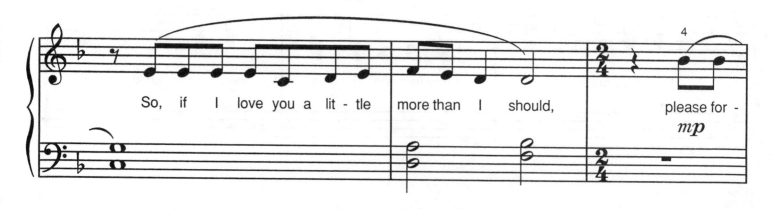

So, if I love you a lit - tle more than I should, please for -

*mp*

# SAID I LOVED YOU . . . BUT I LIED

Composed by MICHAEL BOLTON
and ROBERT JOHN "MUTT" LANGE
*Arranged by ROBERT SCHULTZ*

Said I Loved You . . . But I Lied - 2 - 1
AS006

45

# YOU ARE NOT ALONE

Written and Composed by
R. KELLY
*Arranged by ROBERT SCHULTZ*

# YOU'RE THE INSPIRATION

Words and Music by
DAVID FOSTER and
PETER CETERA
*Arranged by ROBERT SCHULTZ*

**Moderately slow**

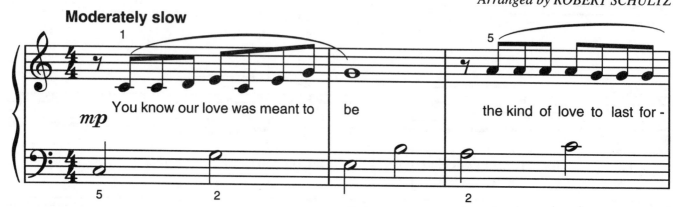

You know our love was meant to be the kind of love to last for-

ev - er; and I want you here with me

from to-night un - til the end of time. You should know

ev - ery-where I go, al - ways on my mind, in my heart, in my soul, ba - by.

*cresc.*

You're the Inspiration - 2 - 1
AS006

You're the mean-ing of my life, you're the in - spi - ra - tion.

You bring mean-ing to my life, you're the in - spi - ra - tion.

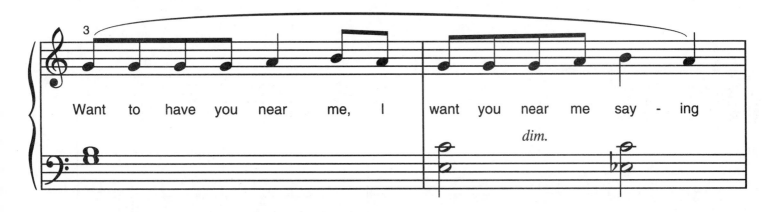

Want to have you near me, I want you near me say - ing

*dim.*

no one needs you more than I need you.

*mp*

*A Greenway Production in Association with 20th Century-Fox TV for ABC-TV*

# BATMAN THEME

By
NEAL HEFTI
*Arranged by ROBERT SCHULTZ*

**Bat rock tempo**

# JEOPARDY THEME

Music by
MERV GRIFFIN
*Arranged by ROBERT SCHULTZ*

**Thoughtfully**

# CHANGING KEYS
# (WHEEL OF FORTUNE THEME)

Music by MERV GRIFFIN
*Arranged by ROBERT SCHULTZ*

Changing Keys - 2 - 1
AS006

# CHARLIE BROWN THEME

By VINCE GUARALDI
*Arranged by ROBERT SCHULTZ*

**Medium swing**

Charlie Brown Theme - 2 - 1
AS006

Charlie Brown Theme - 2 - 2

*From the TV Show "PEANUTS SPECIAL"*

# LINUS AND LUCY

By VINCE GUARALDI
*Arranged by ROBERT SCHULTZ*

*From the Warner Bros. Picture "DAYS OF WINE AND ROSES"*

# DAYS OF WINE AND ROSES

Lyric by
JOHNNY MERCER

Music by
HENRY MANCINI
*Arranged by ROBERT SCHULTZ*

The days _____ of wine and ros - es, _____ laugh and run a - way, _____ like a child at play, _____ through the mead - ow - land to - ward a clos - ing door, a door marked "Nev - er - more," that was - n't there be - fore. _____ The

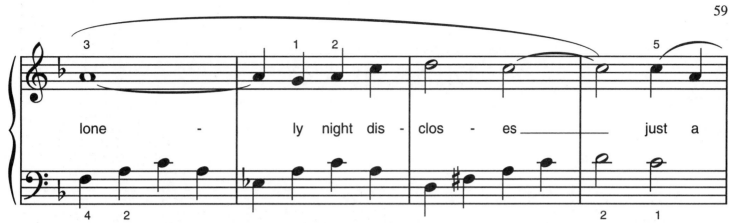

lone - ly night dis - clos - es _____ just a

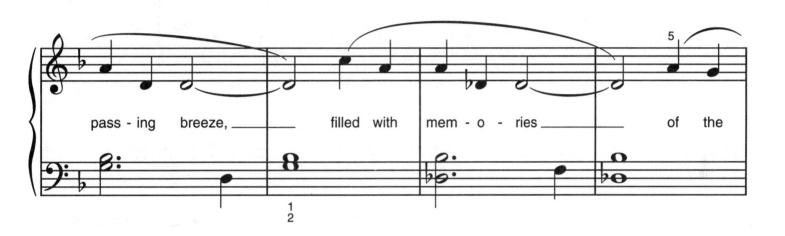

pass - ing breeze, _____ filled with mem - o - ries _____ of the

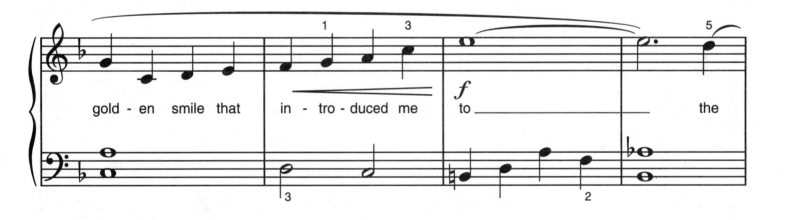

gold - en smile that in - tro - duced me to _____ the

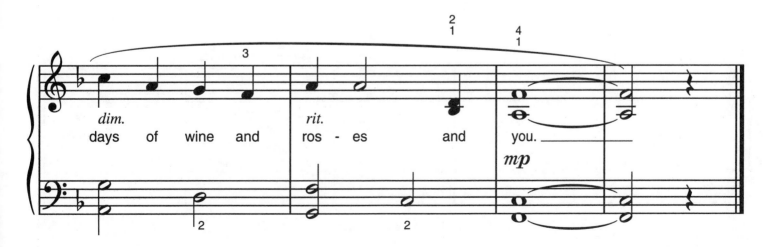

*dim.* days of wine and *rit.* ros - es and you. _____

*Theme Song from the Warner Brothers Production*

# DEAR HEART

Words by
JAY LIVINGSTON
and RAY EVANS

Music by
HENRY MANCINI
*Arranged by ROBERT SCHULTZ*

lone - some town all right! _____ But soon
I'll kiss you hel - lo at our front
door. _____ And dear heart I want you to
know I'll leave your arms _____ nev - er -
more. _____

*rit.*

*p*

Ped. ✻

*From the MGM/UA Motion Picture "THE SECRET OF NIMH"*

# FLYING DREAMS

Lyrics by PAUL WILLIAMS

Music by JERRY GOLDSMITH
*Arranged by* ROBERT SCHULTZ

**Gentle waltz**

Dream by night, wish by day, love be-gins this way. Lov-ing starts when

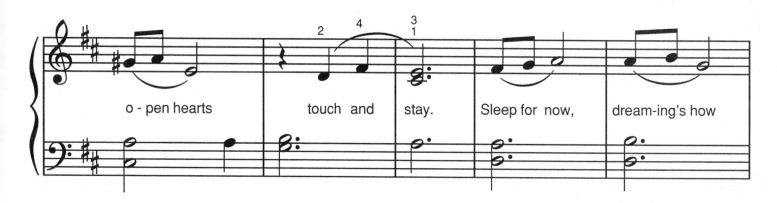

o - pen hearts touch and stay. Sleep for now, dream-ing's how

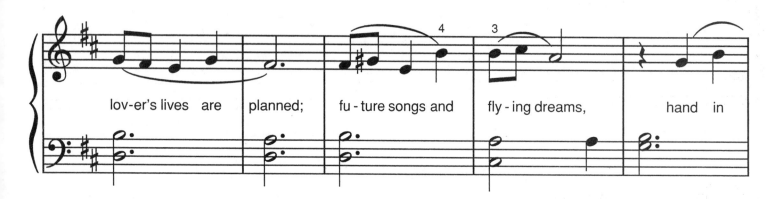

lov-er's lives are planned; fu - ture songs and fly - ing dreams, hand in

hand. Love, it seems, made fly - ing dreams so hearts could soar.

Flying Dreams - 2 - 1
AS006

Verse 2:
Every part is from the heart
And love is still the key.

Verse 3:
Love, it seems, made flying dreams
To bring you home to me.

# I'LL BE THERE FOR YOU
## (Theme from "Friends")

Words by
DAVID CRANE, MARTA KAUFFMAN, ALLEE WILLIS,
PHIL SOLEM and DANNY WILDE

Music by
MICHAEL SKLOFF
*Arranged by ROBERT SCHULTZ*

I'll Be There for You - 3 - 1
AS006

Chorus:

I'll Be There for You - 3 - 2

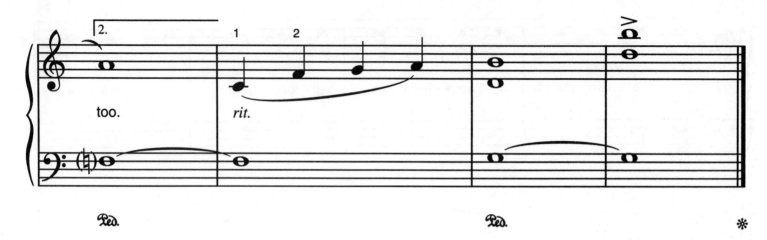

*Verse 2:*
You're still in bed at ten and work began at eight.
You've burned your breakfast, so far, everything is great.
Your mother warned you there'd be days like these,
But she didn't tell you when the world has brought you down to your knees, that
*(To Chorus:)*

*Theme Song from the Television Series*

# PETER GUNN

By HENRY MANCINI
*Arranged by ROBERT SCHULTZ*

**Moderately, with a strong beat**

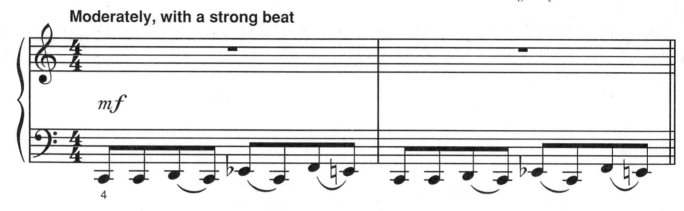

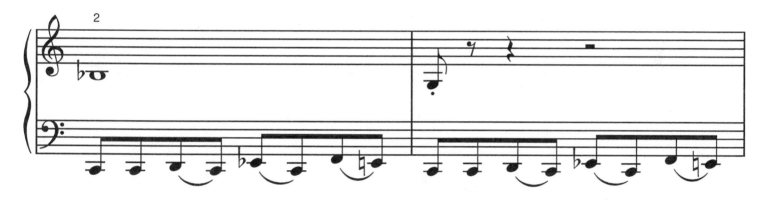

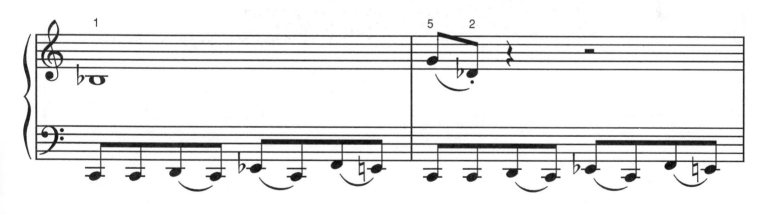

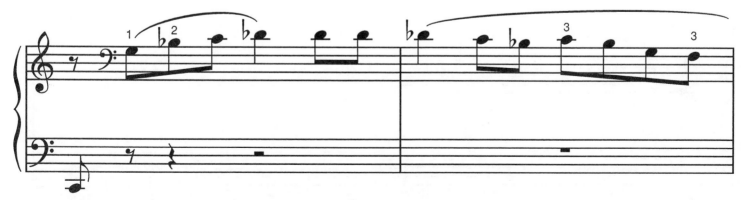

Peter Gunn - 3 - 1
AS006

68

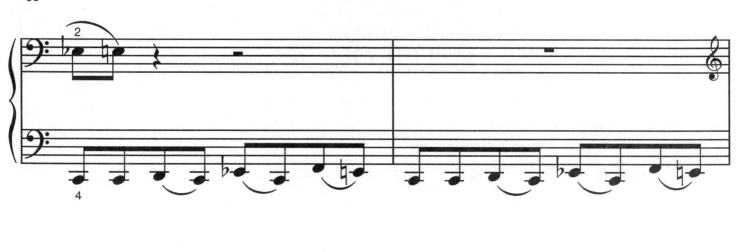

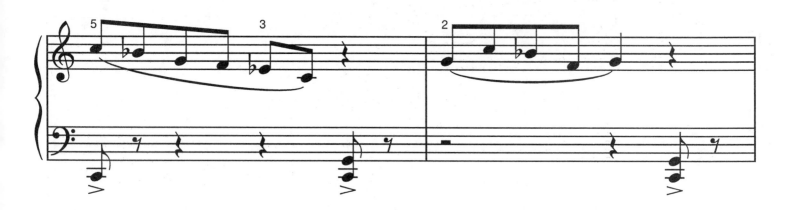

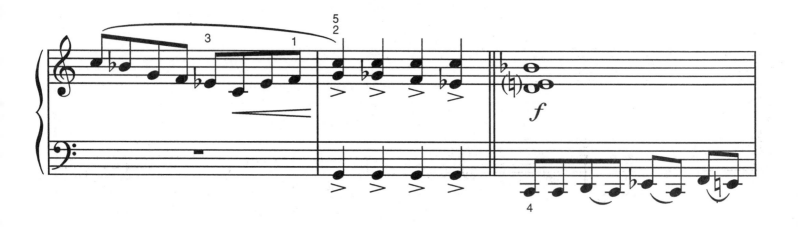

Peter Gunn - 3 - 2

Peter Gunn - 3 - 3

*Columbia Pictures Presents a Mirage/Punch Production: a Sidney Pollack Film "TOOTSIE"*

# IT MIGHT BE YOU
## (Theme from "Tootsie")

Words by
ALAN and MARILYN BERGMAN

Music by
DAVE GRUSIN
*Arranged by ROBERT SCHULTZ*

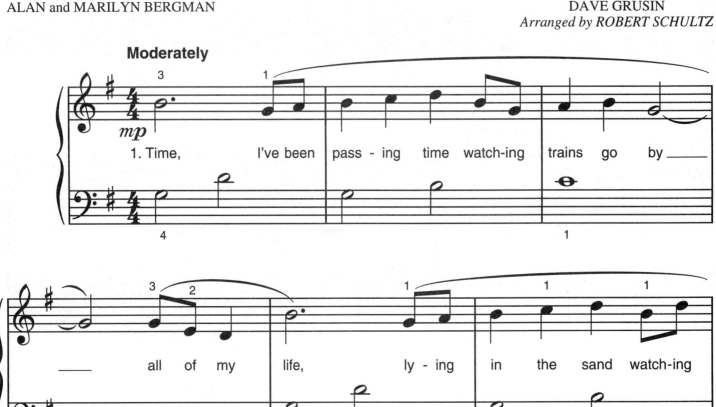

1. Time, I've been pass-ing time watch-ing trains go by ___ all of my life, ly-ing in the sand watch-ing

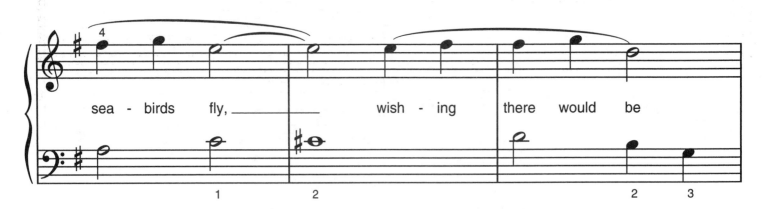

sea - birds fly, ___ wish - ing there would be

*Chorus:*

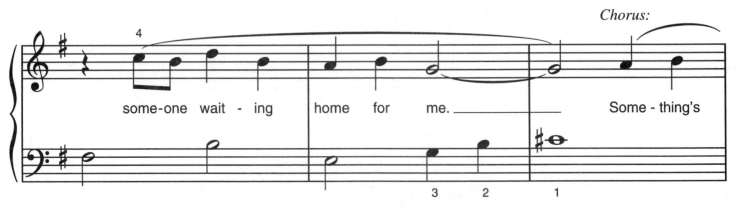

some-one wait - ing home for me. ___ Some - thing's

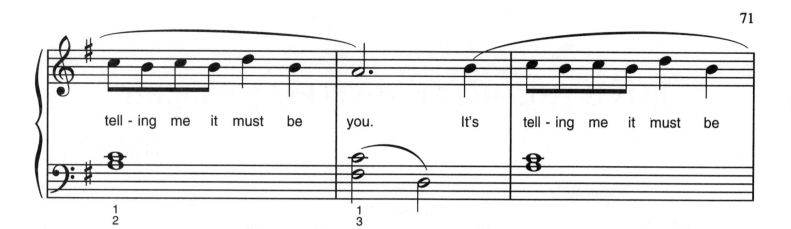

tell - ing me it must be you. It's tell - ing me it must be

you. 2. All of my you, all of my life...

rit. a tempo

*Verse 2:*
All of my life,
Looking back as lovers go walking past,
All of my life,
Wondering how they met and what makes it last.
If I found the place,
Would I recognize the face?
*(To Chorus:)*

*Columbia Pictures Presents a Channel-Lauren Shuler Production*
*A Joel Schumacher Film "ST. ELMO'S FIRE"*

# LOVE THEME FROM ST. ELMO'S FIRE
## (Instrumental)

By DAVID FOSTER
*Arranged by ROBERT SCHULTZ*

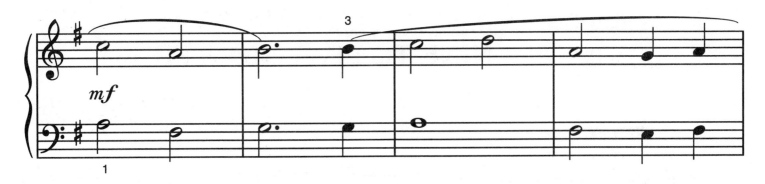

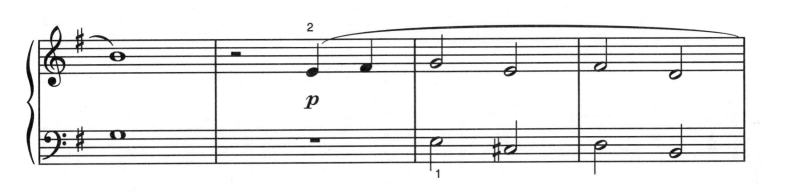

*D.C. al Coda*

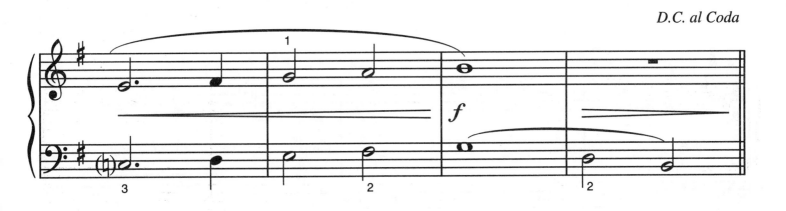

*From the Twentieth Century-Fox Film "9 TO 5"*

# NINE TO FIVE

Words and Music by
DOLLY PARTON

**Very lively**

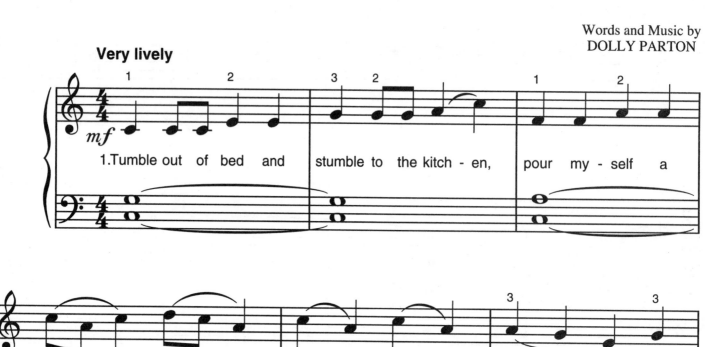

1.Tumble out of bed and stumble to the kitch - en, pour my - self a

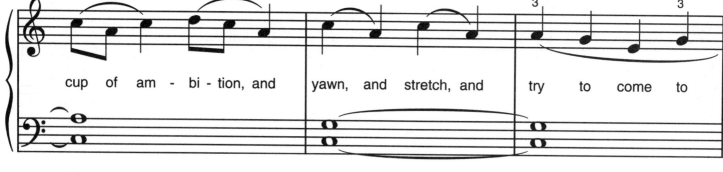

cup of am - bi - tion, and yawn, and stretch, and try to come to

life. Jump in the shower and the

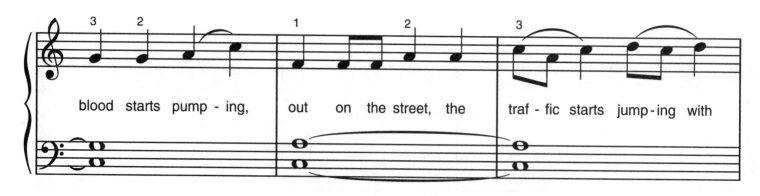

blood starts pump - ing, out on the street, the traf - fic starts jump-ing with

Nine to Five - 3 - 1
AS006

get me!   *mf*

*poco rit.*   *mp*

*Verse 2:*
They let you dream just to watch them shatter,
You're just a step on the boss man's ladder,
But you've got dreams he'll never take away.
In the same boat with a lot of your friends,
Waitin' for the day your ship'll come in,
And the tide's gonna turn, and it's gonna roll your way.

*Chorus 2:*
Working nine to five, for service and devotion;
You would think that I would deserve a fair promotion;
Want to move ahead, but the boss won't seem to let me.
I swear sometimes, that man is out to get me!

20th Century-Fox Presents an Arthur P. Jacobs Production *"DOCTOR DOLITTLE"*

# TALK TO THE ANIMALS

Words and Music by
LESLIE BRICUSSE
Arranged by ROBERT SCHULTZ

*Theme Song from the Mirisch-G&E Production, "THE PINK PANTHER," a United Artists Release*

# THE PINK PANTHER

Music by HENRY MANCINI
*Arranged by ROBERT SCHULTZ*

**Mysteriously**

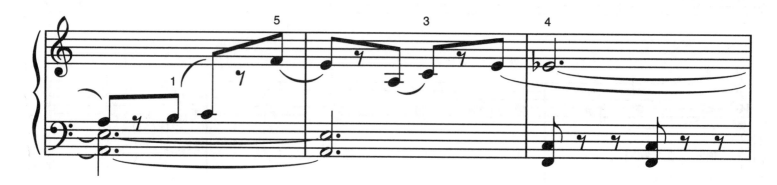

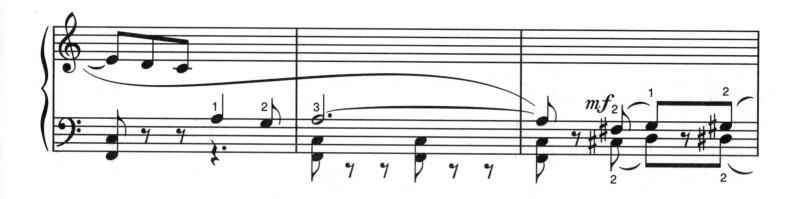

The Pink Panther - 3 - 1
AS006

The Pink Panther - 3 - 2

82

*Metro-Goldwyn-Mayer Presents David Lean's Film "DOCTOR ZHIVAGO"*

# SOMEWHERE, MY LOVE
(Lara's Theme from "DOCTOR ZHIVAGO")

Lyric by
PAUL FRANCIS WEBSTER

Music by
MAURICE JARRE
*Arranged by ROBERT SCHULTZ*

84

all that your heart can hold. _____

Some - day, _____ we'll meet a -

gain my love; _____

some - day, _____ when - ev - er the

spring breaks through. _____

Somewhere, My Love - 3 - 3

*From the 20th Century-Fox Motion Picture "THE SANDPIPER"*

# THE SHADOW OF YOUR SMILE

(Love Theme from "The Sandpiper")

Lyric by
PAUL FRANCIS WEBSTER

Music by
JOHNNY MANDEL
*Arranged by ROBERT SCHULTZ*

The shad-ow of your smile when you are gone will col-or all my dreams and light the dawn. Look in-to my eyes, my love, and see all the love-ly things you are to me.

*From the Lucasfilm Ltd. Production - A Twentieth Century-Fox Release "STAR WARS"*

# STAR WARS
## (Main Title)

Music by
JOHN WILLIAMS
*Arranged by ROBERT SCHULTZ*

Star Wars (Main Title) - 2 - 2

*From the Warner Brothers Production "THE GREAT RACE"*

# THE SWEETHEART TREE

Words by
JOHNNY MERCER

Music by
HENRY MANCINI
*Arranged by ROBERT SCHULTZ*

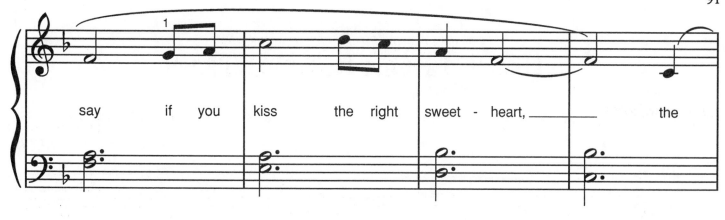

say if you kiss the right sweet - heart,_____ the

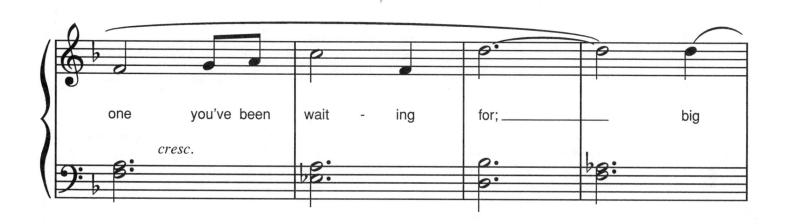

one you've been wait - ing for;_____ big

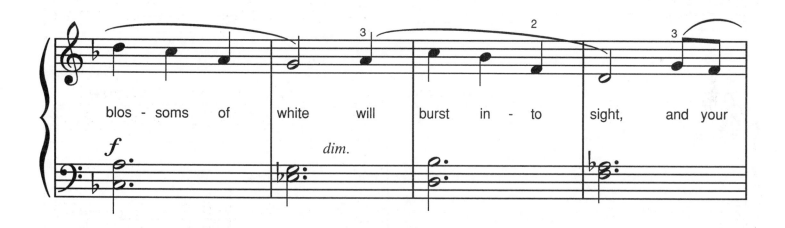

blos - soms of white will burst in - to sight, and your

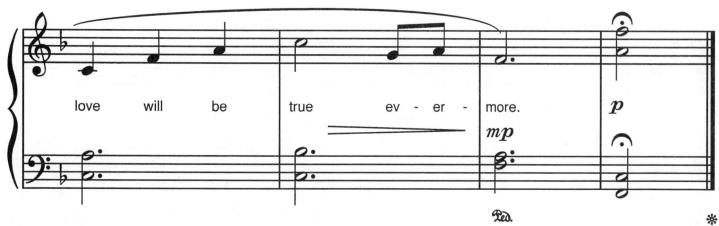

love will be true ev - er - more.

91

*From the Columbia Picture "ICE CASTLES"*

# THEME FROM ICE CASTLES
## (Through the Eyes of Love)

Lyrics by
CAROLE BAYER SAGER

Music by
MARVIN HAMLISCH
*Arranged by ROBERT SCHULTZ*

Please, don't let this feel-ing end, it's ev-ery-thing I

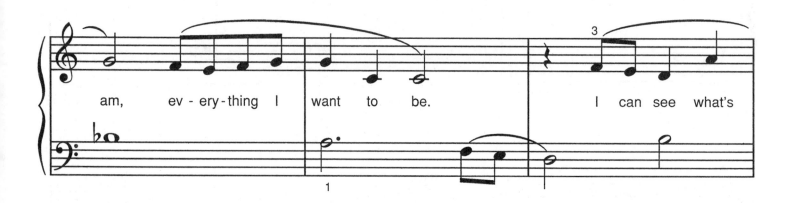

am, ev-ery-thing I want to be. I can see what's

mine now, find-ing out what's true. Since I found

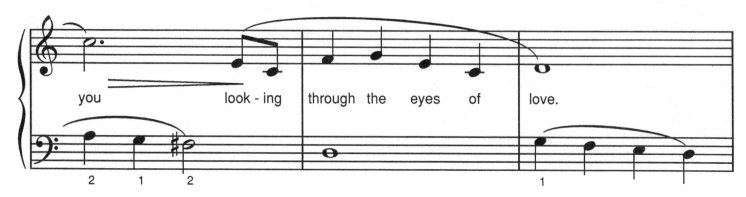

you look-ing through the eyes of love.

Theme from Ice Castles - 2 - 1
AS006

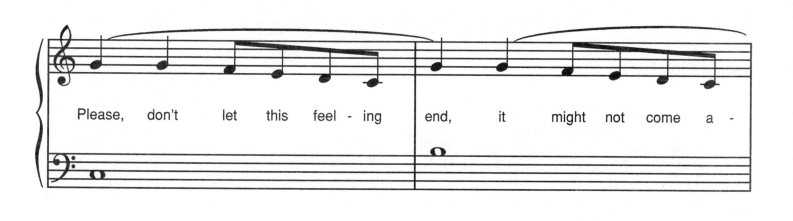

Please, don't let this feel - ing end, it might not come a -

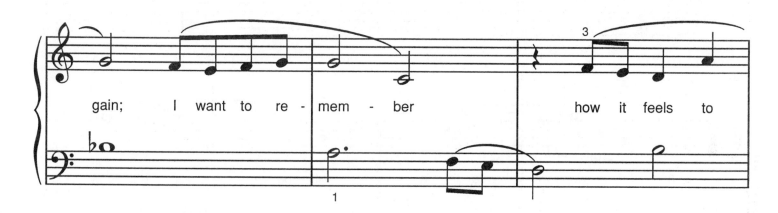

gain; I want to re - mem - ber how it feels to

touch you, how I feel so much since I found

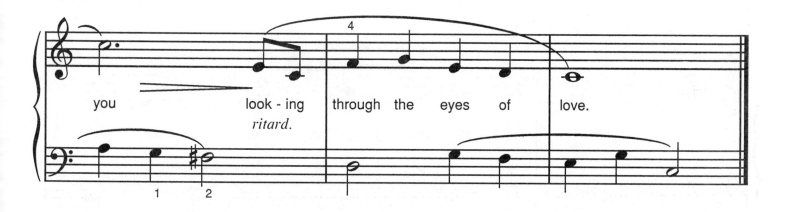

you look - ing through the eyes of love.

*ritard.*

Theme from Ice Castles - 2 - 2

*Theme Song from the Stanley Donen Production, a 20th Century-Fox Film*

# TWO FOR THE ROAD

Words by
LESLIE BRICUSSE

Music by
HENRY MANCINI
*Arranged by ROBERT SCHULTZ*

Two for the Road - 2 - 1
AS006

life    the way we    please. _____ In sum-mer-time the

sun    will shine,    in win - ter we'll drink    sum - mer wine;

and ev-ery day that    you    are mine    will   be   a    love - ly day.

As   long   as    love   still wears   a    smile,   I    know   that we'll   be

two   for the road,   and    that's    a    long,   long    while.    *pp*

*dim.*

Two for the Road - 2 - 2

*From the Motion Picture "AN OFFICER AND A GENTLEMAN"*

# UP WHERE WE BELONG

Words by
WILL JENNINGS

Music by
JACK NITZSCHE
and BUFFY SAINTE-MARIE
*Arranged by ROBERT SCHULTZ*

**Moderately slow**

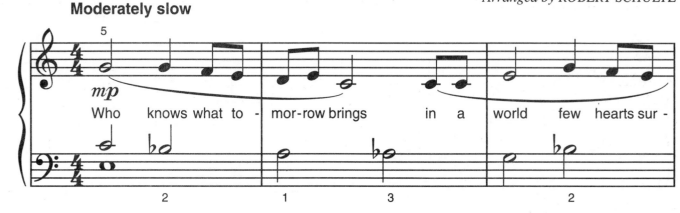

Who knows what to-mor-row brings in a world few hearts sur-

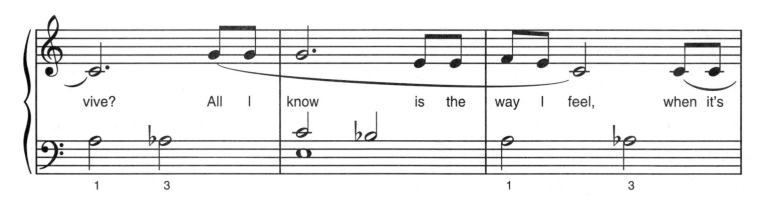

vive? All I know is the way I feel, when it's

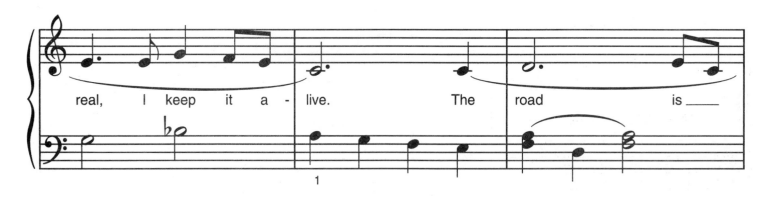

real, I keep it a-live. The road is ___

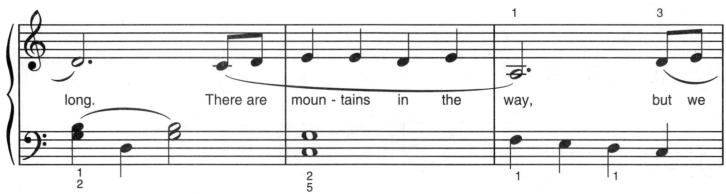

long. There are moun-tains in the way, but we

Up Where We Belong - 2 - 1
AS006

*From the Tristar Pictures Feature Film, "HOOK"*

# WE DON'T WANNA GROW UP

Lyrics by
**LESLIE BRICUSSE**

Music by
**JOHN WILLIAMS**
*Arranged by ROBERT SCHULTZ*

We Don't Wanna Grow Up - 2 - 1
AS006

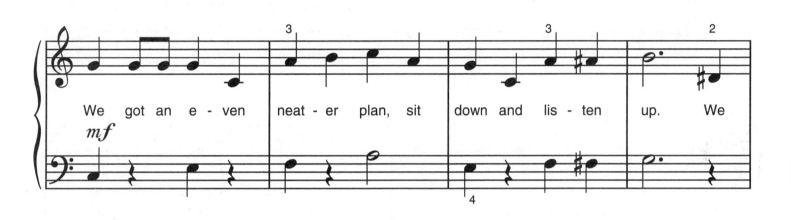

We Don't Wanna Grow Up - 2 - 2

*From the United Artists Motion Picture "THE THOMAS CROWN AFFAIR"*

# THE WINDMILLS OF YOUR MIND

(Theme from "The Thomas Crown Affair")

Lyric by
**ALAN and MARILYN BERGMAN**

Music by
MICHEL LEGRAND
*Arranged by ROBERT SCHULTZ*

Round, like a cir-cle in a spi-ral, like a wheel with-in a
mind. 2.*(see additional lyrics)*

wheel; nev-er end-ing or be-gin-ning on an ev-er spin-ning

reel; like a snow-ball down a moun-tain, or a car-ni-val bal-

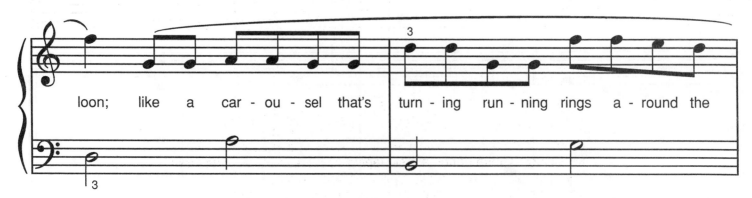

loon; like a car-ou-sel that's turn-ing run-ning rings a-round the

The Windmills of Your Mind - 2 - 1
AS006

moon; like a clock whose hands are sweep-ing past the min-utes of its

face; and the world is like an ap-ple whirl-ing si-lent-ly in

space; like the cir-cles that you find in the wind-mills of your

find in the wind-mills of your mind.

*rit.*       *p*

*Verse 2:*
Like a tunnel that you follow to a tunnel of its own,
Down a hollow to a cavern where the sun has never shone;
Like a door that keeps revolving in a half forgotten dream,
Or the ripples from a pebble someone tosses in a stream;
Like a clock whose hands are sweeping past the minutes of its face;
And the world is like an apple whirling silently in space;
Like the circles that you find in the windmills of your mind.

*From the Columbia Pictures Release "YOU LIGHT UP MY LIFE"*

# YOU LIGHT UP MY LIFE

Words and Music by
JOE BROOKS
*Arranged by ROBERT SCHULTZ*

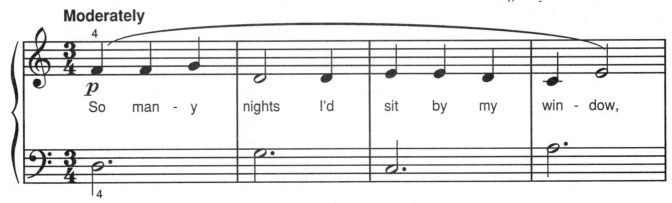

So man - y nights I'd sit by my win - dow,

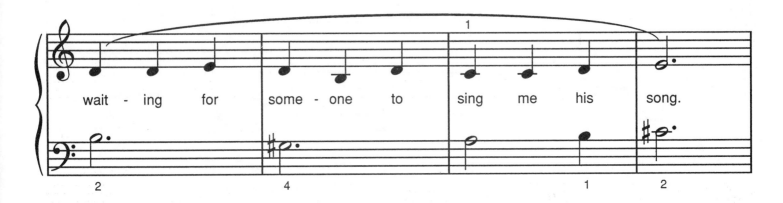

wait - ing for some - one to sing me his song.

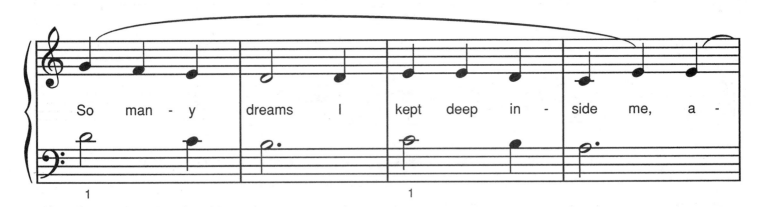

So man - y dreams I kept deep in - side me, a -

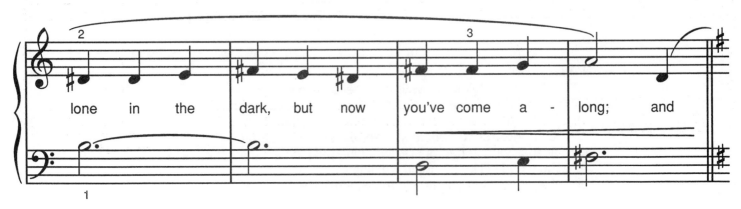

lone in the dark, but now you've come a - long; and

You Light up My Life - 2 - 1
AS006

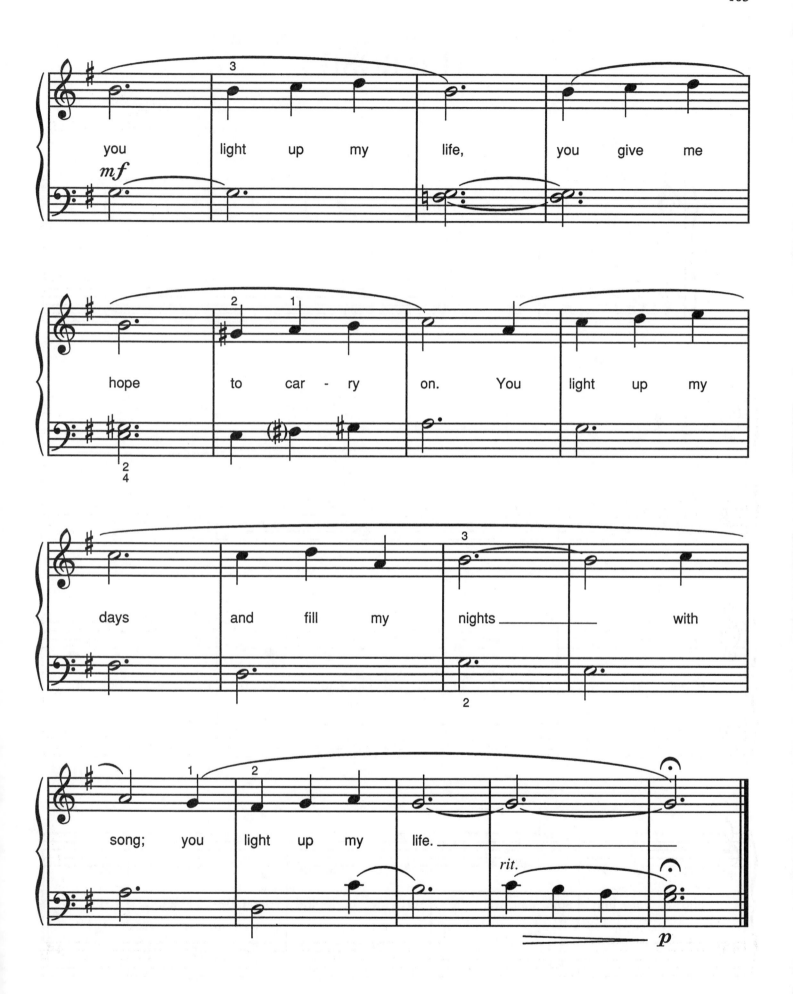

*From the Twentieth Century-Fox Motion Picture "THE ROSE"*

# THE ROSE

Words and Music by
AMANDA McBROOM
*Arranged by ROBERT SCHULTZ*

**Moderately**

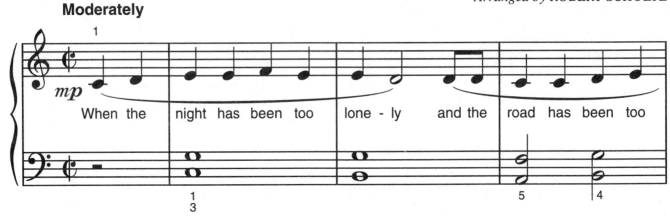

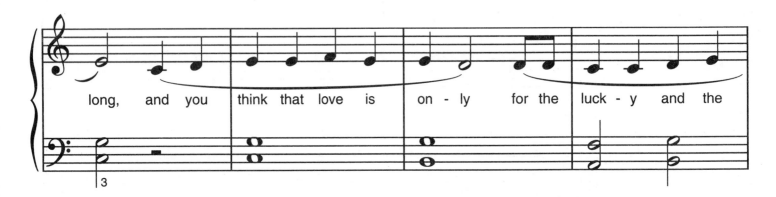

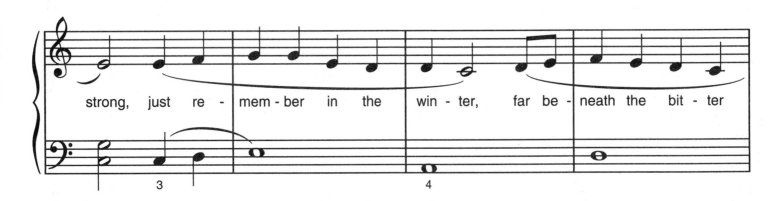

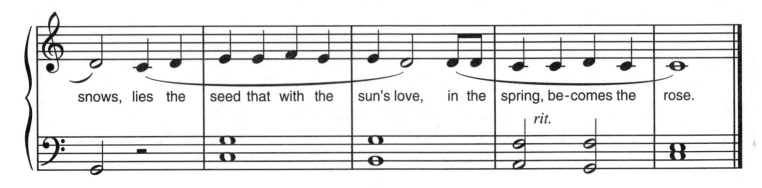

# SONG FROM M*A*S*H
(Suicide Is Painless)

Words and Music by
MIKE ALTMAN and JOHNNY MANDEL
*Arranged by ROBERT SCHULTZ*

*From the Twentieth Century Fox Motion Picture "ANASTASIA"*

# JOURNEY TO THE PAST

Lyrics by
LYNN AHRENS

Music by
STEPHEN FLAHERTY
*Arranged by ROBERT SCHULTZ*

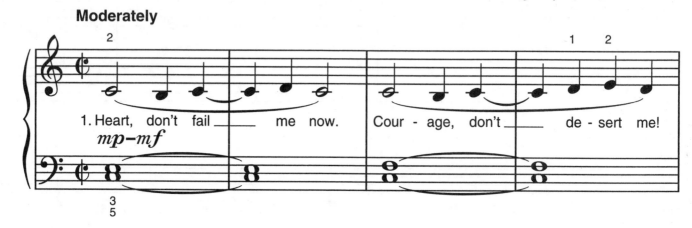

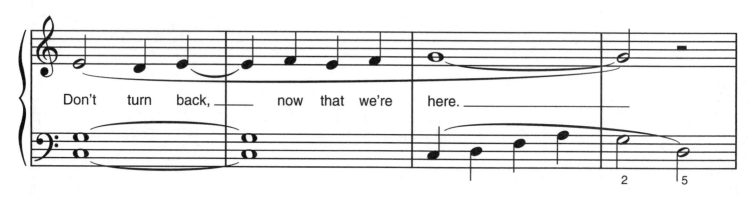

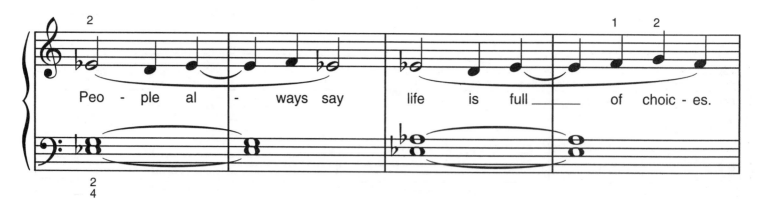

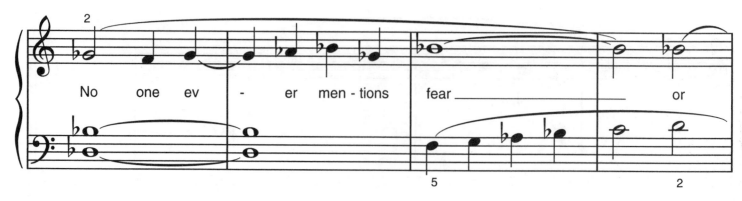

Journey to the Past - 4 - 1
0236B
AS006

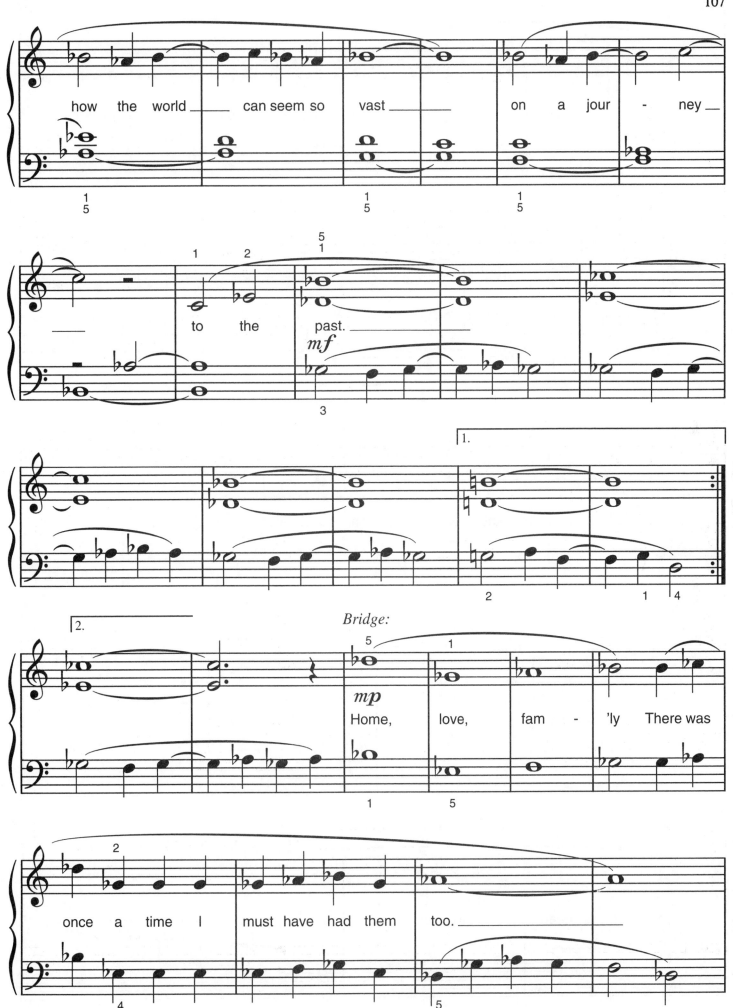

how the world ___ can seem so vast ___ on a jour - ney ___

___ to the past. ___

*mf*

**1.**

**2.** *Bridge:*

*mp*
Home, love, fam - 'ly There was

once a time I must have had them too. ___

108

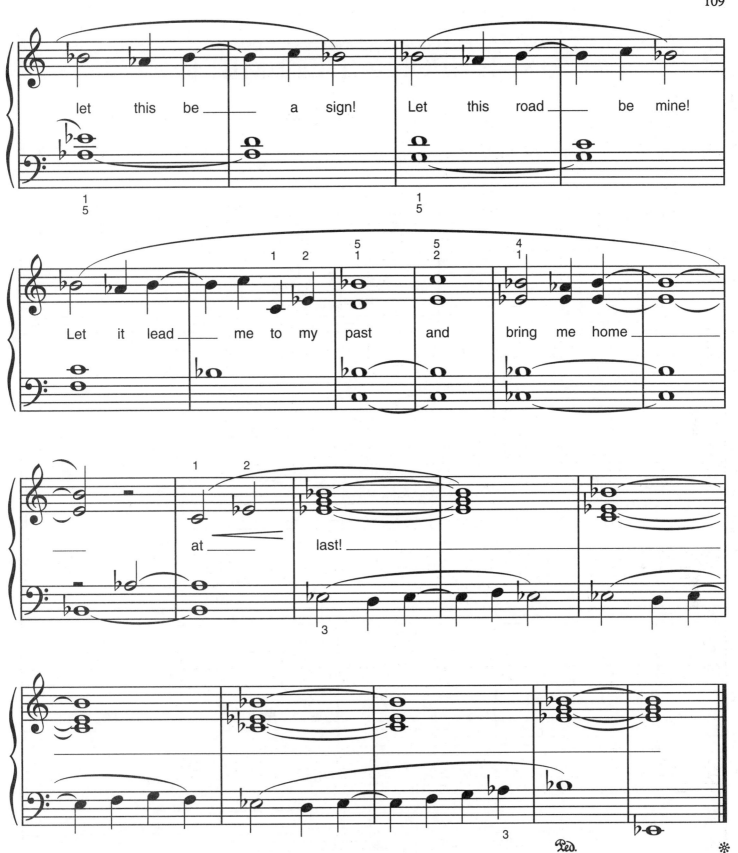

*Verse 2:*
Somewhere down this road I know someone's waiting.
Years of dreams just can't be wrong.
Arms will open wide. I'll be safe and wanted,
Finally home where I belong.
Well, starting now, I'm learning fast,
On this journey to the past.
*(To Bridge:)*

*From the Twentieth Century Fox Motion Picture "ANASTASIA"*

# ONCE UPON A DECEMBER

Lyrics by
LYNN AHRENS

Music by
STEPHEN FLAHERTY
*Arranged by ROBERT SCHULTZ*

**Moderate waltz**

Danc - ing bears, paint - ed wings,

things I al - most re - mem - ber.

*pedal simile*

Once Upon a December - 4 - 1
0236B
AS006

112

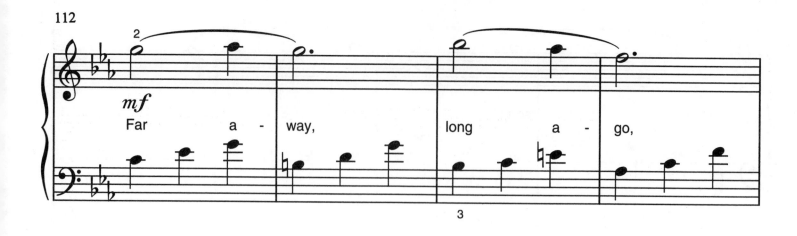

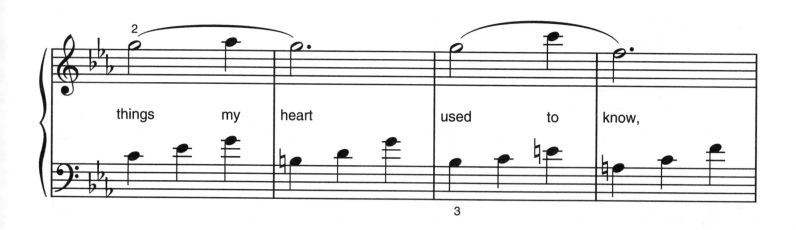

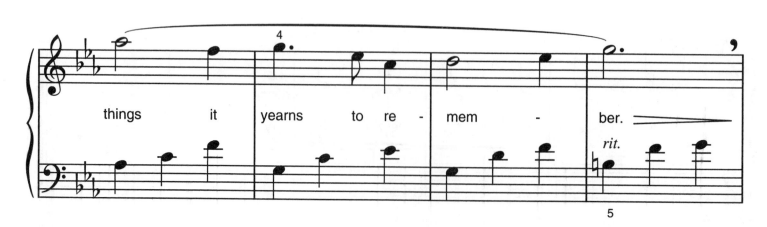

Once Upon a December - 4 - 3
0236B

**A little slower**

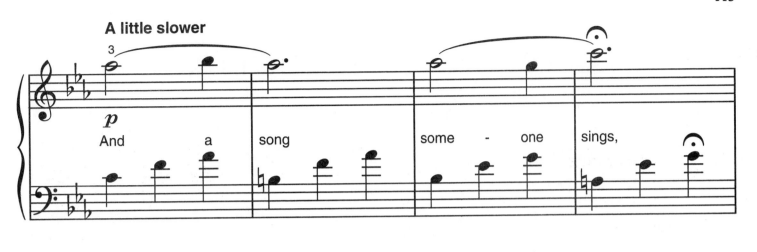

*p*

And    a    song      some - one    sings,

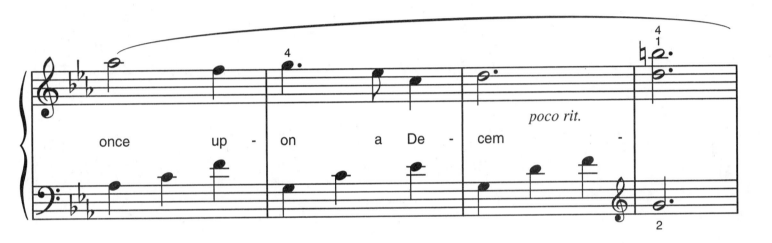

once    up -    on    a    De -    cem

*poco rit.*

ber. _____

*a tempo*

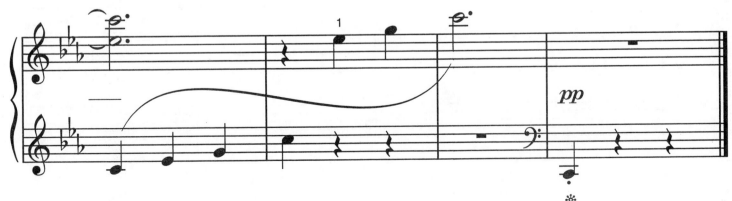

*pp*

Once Upon a December - 4 - 4
0236B

*From the Twentieth Century Fox Motion Picture "ANASTASIA"*

# A RUMOR IN ST. PETERSBURG

Lyrics by
**LYNN AHRENS**

Music by
**STEPHEN FLAHERTY**
*Arranged by ROBERT SCHULTZ*

116

ru - mor   that's part of   our   his - to - ry!

{ They
{ We'll   say her roy - al Grand-ma - ma will

pay a roy - al sum   to   some-one who can bring the Prin-cess   back!

cresc.

2.

find   a   girl   to   play   the   part   and   teach   her   what   to   say,

dress   her   up   and   take   her   to   "Pa - ree!"   Im -

ag - ine   the   re - ward   her   dear   old   Grand - ma - ma   will   pay!   Who

else could pull it off but you and me? We'll be rich! We'll be rich! We'll be

*cresc.*

out! We'll be out! And St. Pe - ters - burg will have some more to talk a - bout *Sssh!*

*f*

*Final Chorus:*

*p*

Have you heard? There's a ru - mor in St. Pe - ters - burg! Have you heard what they're

say - ing on the street? *Hey!* Have you heard? There's a ru - mor in St. Pe - ters - burg!

*f*

Have you heard? Com - rades, what do you sup - pose? A fas - ci - nat - ing mys - ter - y! The

*mf*

118

big-gest con in his-to-ry! _____ The Prin-cess An - a - sta - sia! _____

_____ A - live or dead? Who knows? *Ssshhh!*

*Verse 2:*
A ruble for this painting! It's Romanov, I swear!
Count Yusopov's pajamas! Comrades, buy the pair!
I got them from the palace. It's lined with real fur.
It could be worth a fortune if it belonged to her!

Have you heard? There's a rumor in St. Petersburg!
Have you heard what they're saying in the street?
Although the Tsar did not survive, one daughter may be still alive!
The Princess Anastasia! But please do not repeat!

It's the rumor, the legend, the mystery!
It's the Princess Anastasia who will help us fly!
You and I, friend, will go down in history!
We'll find a girl to play the part and teach her what to say,
Dress her up and take her to "Paree!"
Imagine the reward her dear old Grandmama will pay!
Who else could pull it off but you and me?
We'll be rich! We'll be rich!
We'll be out! We'll be out!
And St. Petersburg will have some more to talk about!
*(To Final Chorus:)*

*From the Twentieth Century Fox Animated Motion Picture "ANASTASIA"*

# IN THE DARK OF THE NIGHT

Lyrics by
LYNN AHRENS

Music by
STEPHEN FLAHERTY
*Arranged by ROBERT SCHULTZ*

In the Dark of the Night - 5 - 1
0236B
AS006

120

Then I o-pened my eyes and the night-mare was me!

I was once the most mys - ti - cal man in all Rus - sia.

When the roy - als be-trayed me, they made a mis - take!

My curse made each of them pay, but one lit - tle girl got a - way!

Lit - tle An - ya, be - ware, Ras - pu - tin's a - wake!

*Chorus:*

In the dark of the night, e - vil will find her!

In the dark of the night, just be - fore dawn. Re -

venge ____ will be sweet when the curse ____ is com-plete!

In the dark of the night, she'll be gone! *dim.*

1.

2.

through!

122

In the Dark of the Night - 5 - 4
0236B

shine!     Find her now! Yes,    fly ev - er fast - er!

In the dark of the night! In the dark of the night! In the dark of the night! *She'll be*

*cresc.*

*mine!*

*rit.*

*Verse 2:*
I can feel that my powers are slowly returning.
Tie my sash and a dash of cologne for that smell.
As the pieces fall into place,
I'll see her crawl into place.
Dasvidanya, Anya, your grace, farewell!

*Chorus 2:*
In the dark of the night, terror will strike her!
In the dark of the night, evil will brew!
Soon she will feel that her nightmares are real!
In the dark of the night, she'll be through!
*(To 2nd ending)*

*From the Twentieth Century Fox Motion Picture "ANASTASIA"*

# LEARN TO DO IT

Lyrics by
LYNN AHRENS

Music by
STEPHEN FLAHERTY
*Arranged by ROBERT SCHULTZ*

Was I wild? Wrote the book! But you'd be - have when your fa - ther gave that look! I -

*mf*

mag-ine how it was! Your long for-got-ten past! We've lots and lots to teach you and the

time is go-ing fast!

*f*

1. Now,
*mp*

*Verse:*

shoul-ders back and stand up tall. And do not walk, but try to float. I

feel a lit - tle fool-ish. Am I float - ing? Like a lit - tle boat! You

125

Learn to Do It - 6 - 2
0236B

126

Learn to Do It - 6 - 3
0236B

128

Chorus:

fat! And I re-call his yel-low cat.

I don't believe we told her that.                    1. If

you can learn to do it,          I can learn to do it!

Don't know how you knew it.      I sim-ply knew it!   Sud-den-ly I feel like

some-one new!          An - ya, you're a dream come true!          2. If

Learn to Do It - 6 - 5
0236B

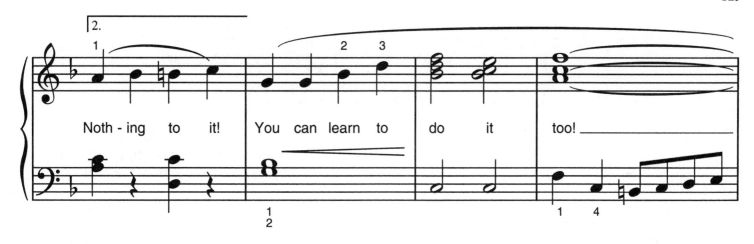

Noth - ing    to    it!    You  can  learn  to    do    it    too! _____

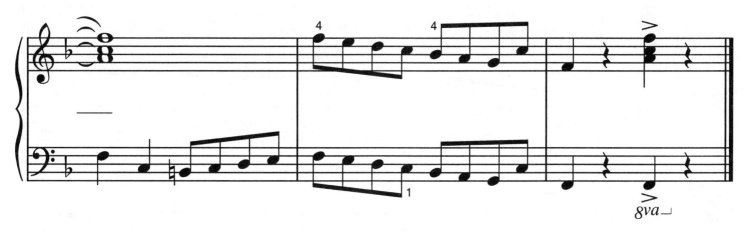

*8va*

*Verse 2:*
Now, elbows in and sit up straight.
And never slurp the stroganoff.
I never cared for stroganoff.
She said that like a Romanov!
The samovar. The caviar. Desert and then goodnight!
Not until you get this right!

*Chorus 2:*
If I can learn to do it, you can learn to do it.
Pull yourself together and you'll pull through it!
Tell yourself it's easy and it's true!
You can learn to do it too!
*(to 2nd ending)*

*Final Chorus:*
If I can learn to do it, you can learn to do it!
Pull yourself together and you'll pull through it!
Tell yourself it's easy and it's true!
You can learn to do it!
Nothing to it!
You can learn to do it too!

*From the Twentieth Century Fox Animated Motion Picture "ANASTASIA"*

# PARIS HOLDS THE KEY
# (TO YOUR HEART)

Words and Music by
LYNN AHRENS and STEPHEN FLAHERTY
*Arranged by ROBERT SCHULTZ*

*Pronounced "Par-ee" throughout.

Wel - come, my friends, to *Par - is. Here, have a flow - er on me. For - get where you're from. You're in France! Chil-dren, come! I'll show you that French joie de vivre! 1. Par - is holds the key to your

Paris Holds the Key (To Your Heart) - 4 - 1
0236B
AS006

*To Coda* ⊕

132

Paris Holds the Key (To Your Heart) - 4 - 3
0236B

Verse 2:
Paris holds the key to her past,
Yes, Princess, I've found you at last.
No more pretend. You'll be gone. That's the end...

Paris holds the key to your heart!
You'll be très jolie and so smart!
Come dance through the night and forget all your woes!
The city of light! Where a rose is a rose!
And one never knows what will start!
Paris holds the key to her heart!

Paris Holds the Key (To Your Heart) - 4 - 4
0236B

*From the Broadway Musical "FIDDLER ON THE ROOF"*

# TRADITION

Lyrics by
**SHELDON HARNICK**

Music by
**JERRY BOCK**
*Arranged by ROBERT SCHULTZ*

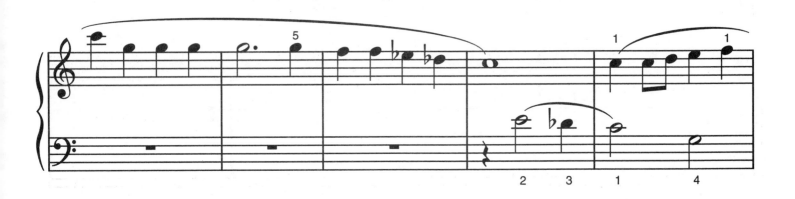

Tradition - 8 - 1
AS006

pa - pa, _____ the pa - pa,

tra - di - tion. _

Who must know the way to make a prop - er home, a
*mp*

qui - et home, a ko - sher home? Who must raise a fam - i - ly and

run the home so pa - pa's free to read the ho - ly book? The
*mf*

139

Tradition - 8 - 6

*From the Broadway Musical "FIDDLER ON THE ROOF"*

# SABBATH PRAYER

Lyrics by
**SHELDON HARNICK**

Music by
**JERRY BOCK**
*Arranged by ROBERT SCHULTZ*

**Moderately slow, reverently**

Sabbath Prayer - 3 - 1
AS006

144

*Sabbath Prayer - 3 - 3*

*From the Broadway Musical "FIDDLER ON THE ROOF"*

# MATCHMAKER

Lyrics by
**SHELDON HARNICK**

Music by
**JERRY BOCK**
*Arranged by ROBERT SCHULTZ*

Matchmaker - 3 - 1
AS006

well, I would-n't hol-ler if he were as hand-some as

an-y-thing! *mf* Match-mak-er, match-mak-er, make me a

match, find me a find, catch me a catch. Night af-ter

night in the dark I'm a-lone, so find me a match

of my own. *p*

Matchmaker - 3 - 3

*From the Broadway Musical "FIDDLER ON THE ROOF"*

# SUNRISE, SUNSET

Lyrics by
SHELDON HARNICK

Music by
JERRY BOCK
*Arranged by ROBERT SCHULTZ*

Sunrise, Sunset - 4 - 1
AS006

When did they?

When did she get to be a beau - ty?

When did she grow to be so tall?

Was - n't it yes - ter - day when they were

small?

*dim.*

*Sunrise, Sunset - 4 - 2*

_____ fly the years. One sea-son fol-low-ing an-

oth - er, la - den with hap-pi-ness and tears. _____

*dim.*

la - den with hap-pi-ness and

*mp*

tears. _____

*a tempo*

*rit.*

*Verse 2:*
What words of wisdom can I give them?
How can I help to ease their way?
Now they must learn from one another,
Day by day.
They look so natural together,
Just like two newlyweds should be.
Is there a canopy in store for me?
*(To Chorus:)*

*From the Broadway Musical "FIDDLER ON THE ROOF"*

# TO LIFE

Lyrics by
**SHELDON HARNICK**

Music by
**JERRY BOCK**
*Arranged by ROBERT SCHULTZ*

To Life - 4 - 1
AS006

chai - im. _____ L' - chai - im, L' - chai - im, to

life. Life has a way of con - fus - ing us.

Bless - ing and bruis - ing us. Drink, L' - chai - im, to

life. *mp* God would like us to be

joy - ful, e - ven when our hearts lie pant - ing on the floor.

To Life - 4 - 2

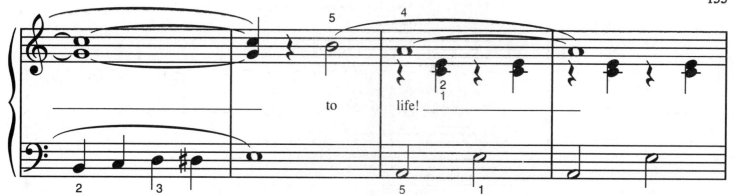

to life!

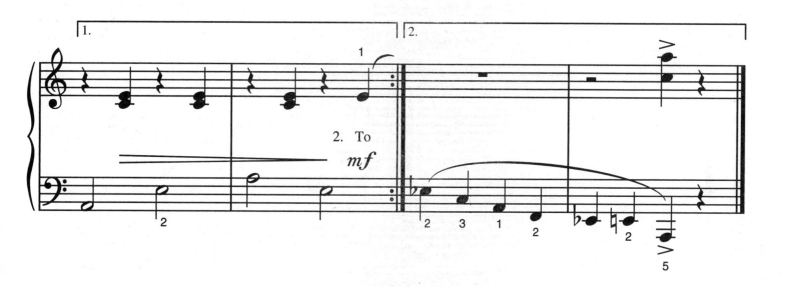

2. To
*mf*

*Verse 2:*
To Lazar Wolfe. To Tevye.
To Tzeitel, your daughter. My wife.
May all you futures be pleasant ones,
Not like our present ones.
Drink, L'chaim.
To life, to life, L'chaim.
L'chaim, L'chaim, to life.
It takes a wedding to make us say:
Let's live another day.
Drink, L'chaim, to life.

We'll raise a glass and sip a drop of schnapps
In honor of the great, good luck that favored you.
We know that when good fortune favors two such men,
It stands to reason we deserve it too.

To us and our good fortune!
Be happy. Be healthy. Long life!
And if our good fortune never comes,
Here's to whatever comes.
Drink, L'chaim, to life!

# DON'T IT MAKE MY BROWN EYES BLUE

Words and Music by
RICHARD LEIGH
*Arranged by ROBERT SCHULTZ*

Don't It Make My Brown Eyes Blue - 3 - 1
AS006

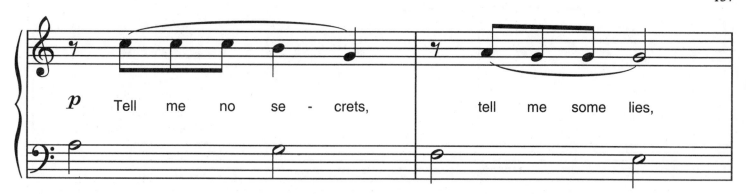

*p*  Tell me no se - crets, tell me some lies,

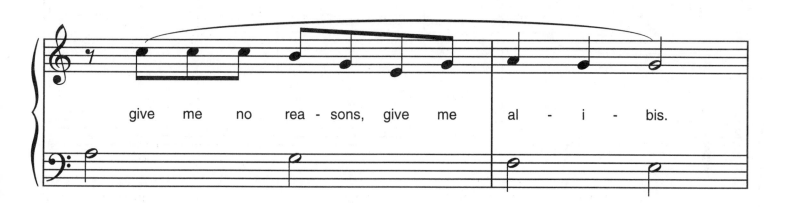

give me no rea - sons, give me al - i - bis.

Tell me you love me, don't let me cry,

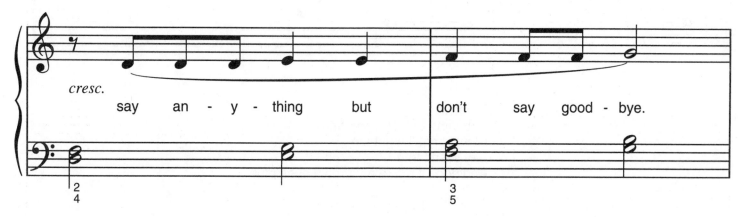

*cresc.*  say an - y - thing but don't say good - bye.

*mf* Did - n't mean to treat you bad, \_\_\_ did - n't know just

what I had, but hon - ey, now I do, and

don't it make my brown eyes, *cresc.* don't it make my brown eyes,

*f* don't it make my brown eyes blue.

*Verse 2:*
I'll be fine until you're gone,
I'll just cry all night long,
Say it isn't true;
And don't it make my brown eyes blue.

# THE HOUSE OF THE RISING SUN

Words and Music by
ALAN PRICE
*Arranged by ROBERT SCHULTZ*

*Verse 2:*
My mother is a tailor, she sews those new blue jeans;
My father is a gambling man down in New Orleans.

# HEY! BABY!

Words and Music by
MARGARET COBB and
BRUCE CHANNEL
*Arranged by ROBERT SCHULTZ*

Moderate shuffle

Hey ____ hey ____ ba - by, ____ I want to know ____ if you'll be my girl.

girl. ____ When I saw you walk-ing

Hey! Baby! - 2 - 1
AS006

# THE LION SLEEPS TONIGHT

New Lyric and Revised Music by
**GEORGE DAVID WEISS, HUGO PERETTI**
and **LUIGI CREATORE**
*Arranged by ROBERT SCHULTZ*

way.        Ah - we-mo-weh, ah - we - mo-weh, ah -        we-mo-weh, ah - we-mo-weh, ah -

we-mo-weh, ah-we-mo-weh, ah - we-mo-weh, ah-we-mo-weh, ah - we-mo-weh, ah-we-mo-weh, ah -

we-mo-weh, ah-we-mo-weh, ah - we-mo-weh, ah-we-mo-weh, ah - we-mo-weh, ah-we-mo-weh.

**Slower (even ♪)**

*poco rit.*

*Verse 2:*
Near the village, the peaceful village, the lion sleeps tonight.
Near the village, the quiet village, the lion sleeps tonight.

*Verse 3:*
Hush, my darling, don't fear, my darling, the lion sleeps tonight.
Hush, my darling, don't fear, my darling, the lion sleeps tonight.

# MUSTANG SALLY

Words and Music by
BONNY RICE
*Arranged by ROBERT SCHULTZ*

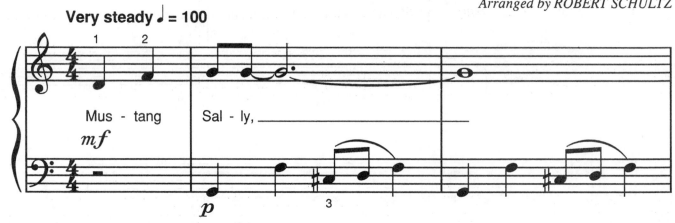

Mus - tang Sal - ly,

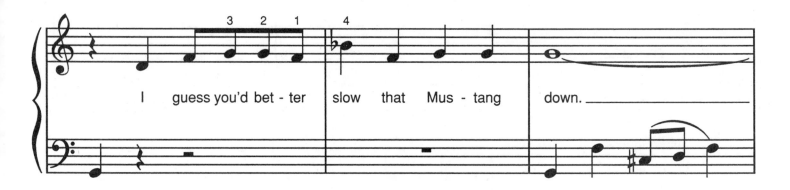

I guess you'd bet - ter slow that Mus - tang down.

Mus - tang

Sal - ly, I think you'd bet - ter

Mustang Sally - 2 - 1
AS006

slow your Mus - tang down. _____

Well, you've been run - nin' all o - ver

town, ___ I guess I'll have to put your flat feet on the

ground. _____

# PUT A LITTLE LOVE IN YOUR HEART

Words and Music by
JIMMY HOLIDAY, RANDY MYERS
and JACKIE DE SHANNON
*Arranged by ROBERT SCHULTZ*

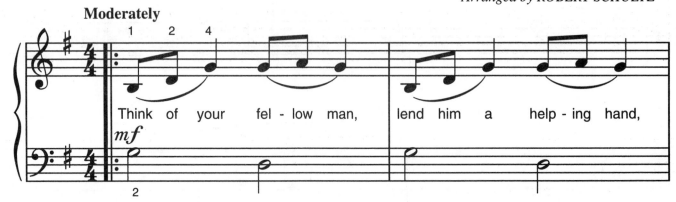

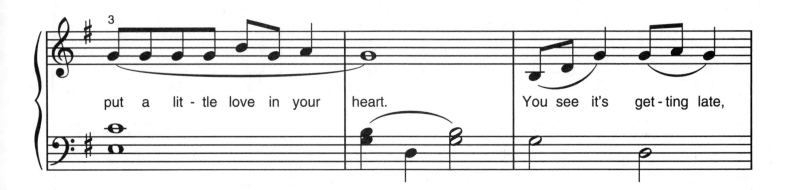

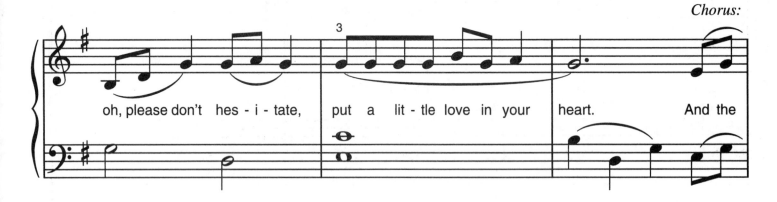

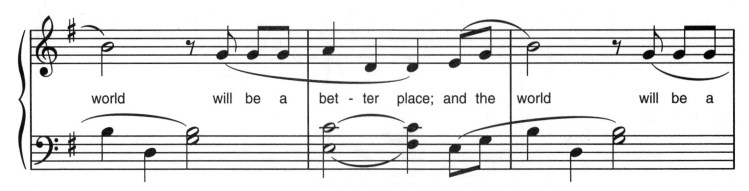

*Put a Little Love in Your Heart - 2 - 1*
AS006

**Verse 2:**
Another day goes by, and still the children cry,
Put a little love in your heart.
If you want the world to know, we won't let hatred grow,
Put a little love in your heart.
*(To Chorus:)*

**Verse 3:**
Take a good look around, and if you're looking down,
Put a little love in your heart.
I hope when you decide, kindness will be your guide.
Put a little love in your heart.
*(To Chorus:)*

# (SHE'S) SOME KIND OF WONDERFUL
## a/k/a SOME KIND OF WONDERFUL

Words and Music by
J. ELLISON
*Arranged by ROBERT SCHULTZ*

**Verse 2:**
When she holds me in her arms, she sets my soul on fire.
Oh, when my baby kisses me, she fills my heart with desire.
When she wraps her lovin' arms around me, almost drives me out of my mind,
I feel a burnin' little feelin' inside of me, chills run up and down my spine.
My baby, she's alright. My baby's clean out of sight.
Don't you know that she's some kind of wonderful.
Yes, she is some kind of wonderful.

# SUNNY

Words and Music by
**BOBBY HEBB**
*Arranged by ROBERT SCHULTZ*

*Verse 2:*
Sunny, thank you for the sunshine bouquet.
Sunny, thank you for the love you've brought my way.
You gave to me your all and all,
Now I feel ten feet tall,
Sunny, one so true, I love you.

*Verse 3:*
Sunny, thank you for the truth you've let me see.
Sunny, thank you for the facts from A to Z.
My life was torn like wind-blown sand,
Then a rock was formed when we held hands,
Sunny, one so true, I love you.

*Verse 4:*
Sunny, thank you for the smile upon your face.
Sunny, thank you for the gleam that flows with grace.
You're my spark of nature's fire,
You're my sweet complete desire,
Sunny, one so true, I love you.

Sunny - 2 - 2

# WE'VE ONLY JUST BEGUN

Words by
PAUL WILLIAMS

Music by
ROGER NICHOLS
*Arranged by ROBERT SCHULTZ*

We've on - ly just be - gun to live, _____

_____ white lace and prom - is - es, a kiss for luck, we're

on our way. _____ Be - fore the ris - ing

We've Only Just Begun - 2 - 1
AS006

sun    we    fly, _____ so man-y roads to choose,

we start out walking and learn to run. _____ And yes, we've just be -

gun.      We've on - ly just be - gun. *dim.*

We've Only Just Begun - 2 - 2

# OLD TIME ROCK & ROLL

Words and Music by
GEORGE JACKSON and THOMAS E. JONES III
*Arranged by ROBERT SCHULTZ*

# AULD LANG SYNE

TRADITIONAL
*Arranged by ROBERT SCHULTZ*

# AMERICA
## (My Country 'Tis of Thee)

Words by
REV. SAMUEL F. SMITH

Music by
HENRY CAREY
*Arranged by ROBERT SCHULTZ*

# AMERICA THE BEAUTIFUL

Words by
KATHERINE LEE BATES

Music by
SAMUEL A. WARD
*Arranged by ROBERT SCHULTZ*

# GREENSLEEVES

TRADITIONAL ENGLISH
*Arranged by ROBERT SCHULTZ*

**Moderately flowing**

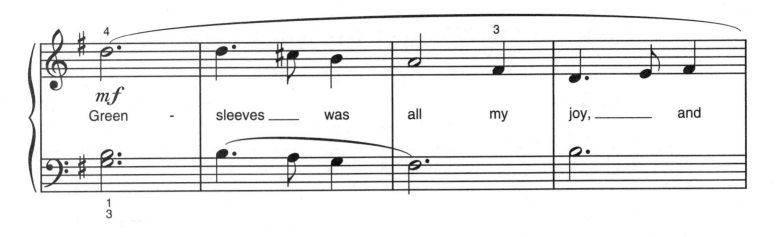

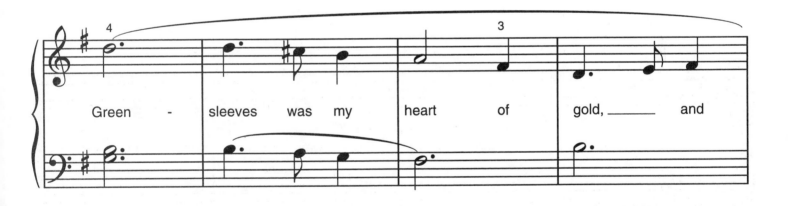

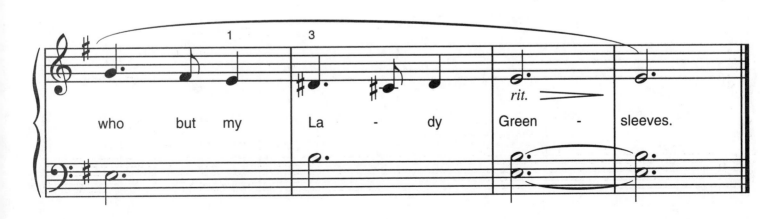

# DID YOU EVER SEE A LASSIE?

SINGING GAME
*Arranged by ROBERT SCHULTZ*

# HEY DIDDLE DIDDLE

NONSENSE SONG
*Arranged by ROBERT SCHULTZ*

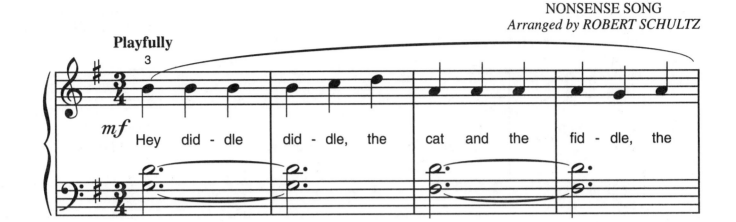

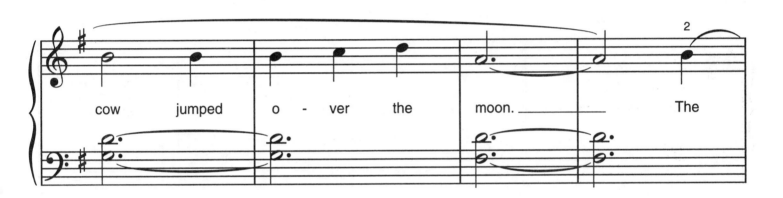

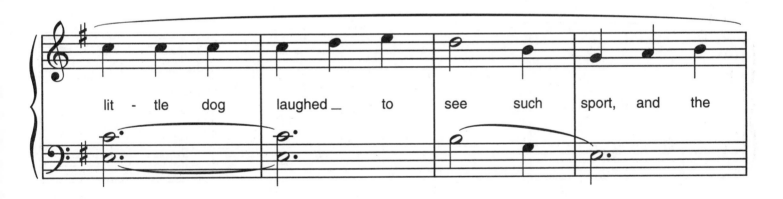

# HOME ON THE RANGE

TRADITIONAL
*Arranged by ROBERT SCHULTZ*

Home on the Range - 2 - 1

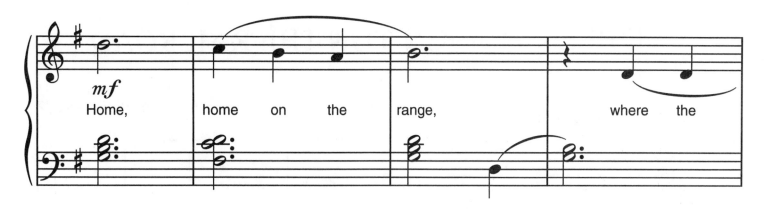

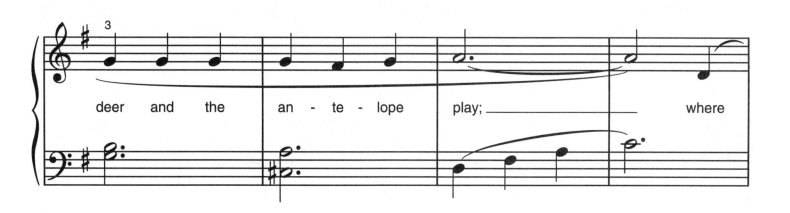

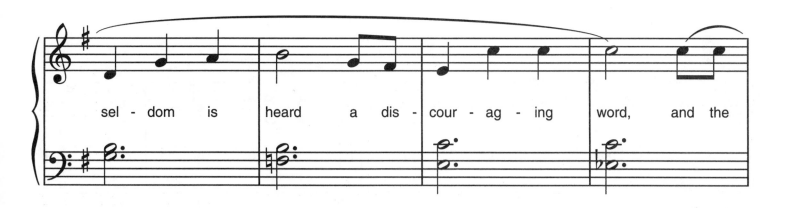

Home on the Range - 2 - 2

# I'VE BEEN WORKING ON THE RAILROAD

TRADITIONAL
*Arranged by ROBERT SCHULTZ*

**Briskly, with spirit**

# ROCK-A-BYE BABY

TRADITIONAL
*Arranged by ROBERT SCHULTZ*

Rock - a - bye ba - by, on the tree - top,

when the wind blows, the cra - dle will rock.

When the bough breaks, the cra - dle will fall, and

down will come ba - by, cra - dle and all.

# MY BONNIE LIES OVER THE OCEAN

TRADITIONAL
*Arranged by ROBERT SCHULTZ*

**Moderately, very flowing**

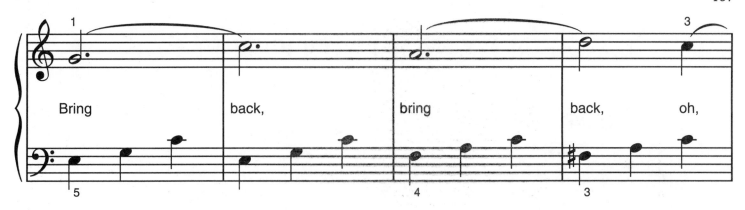

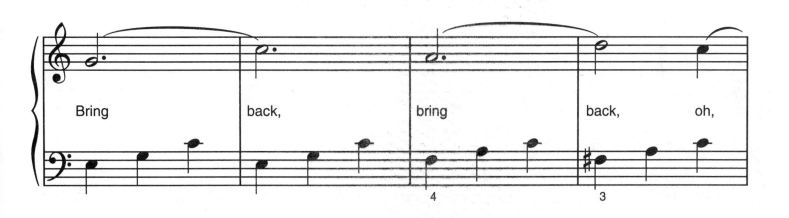

My Bonnie Lies Over the Ocean - 2 - 2

# POLLY WOLLY DOODLE

TRADITIONAL
*Arranged by ROBERT SCHULTZ*

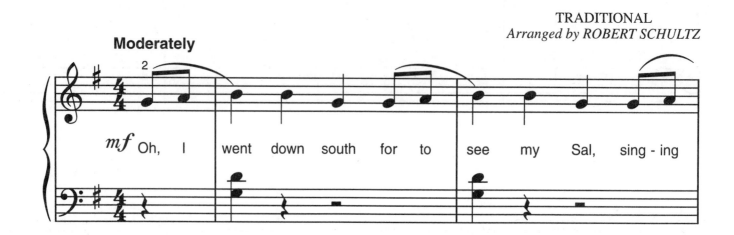

Oh, I went down south for to see my Sal, sing-ing

Pol - ly Wol - ly Doo - dle all the day. My ___

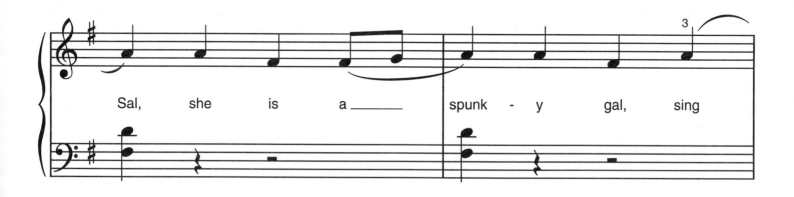

Sal, she is a ___ spunk - y gal, sing

Pol - ly Wol - ly Doo - dle all the day. Fare thee

Polly Wolly Doodle - 2 - 1

well,　　　　　　　fare thee well,　　　　　　　fare thee

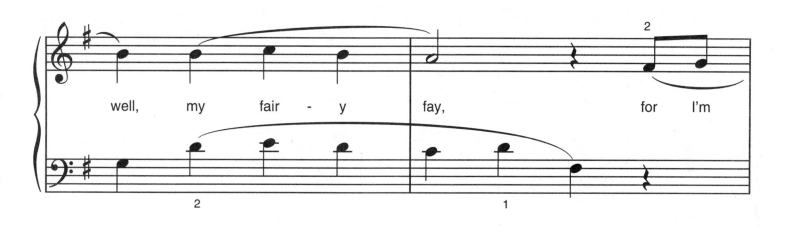

well, my fair - y fay,　　　　　for I'm

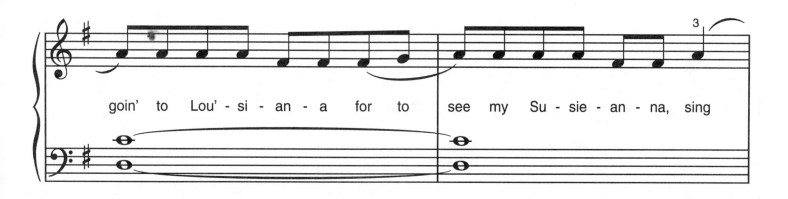

goin' to Lou'- si - an - a for to see my Su - sie - an - na, sing

Pol - ly Wol - ly Doo - dle all the day.

# SHE'LL BE COMIN' 'ROUND THE MOUNTAIN

TRADITIONAL
*Arranged by ROBERT SCHULTZ*

# SHENANDOAH

TRADITIONAL
*Arranged by ROBERT SCHULTZ*

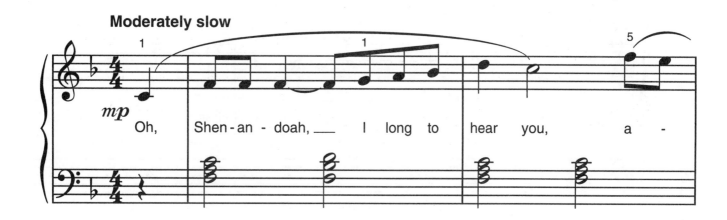

*mp*

Oh, Shen-an-doah, __ I long to hear you, a-

way, __ you roll-ing riv-er. Oh, Shen-an-doah, _ I long to hear you, a-

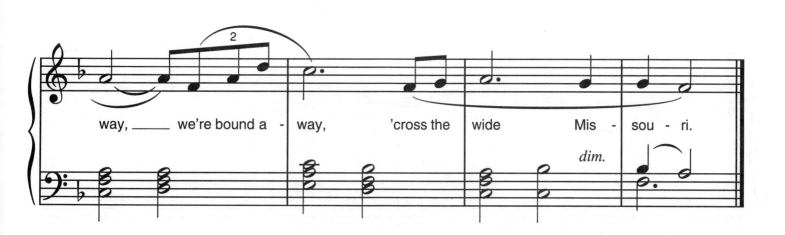

way, __ we're bound a-way, 'cross the wide Mis-sou-ri.

*dim.*

# WAYFARING STRANGER

TRADITIONAL
*Arranged by ROBERT SCHULTZ*

**Slowly, sadly**

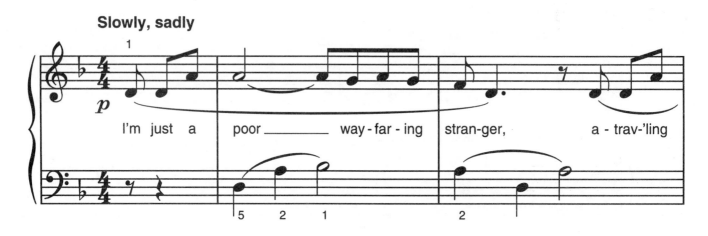

I'm just a poor _____ way-far-ing stran-ger, a-trav-'ling

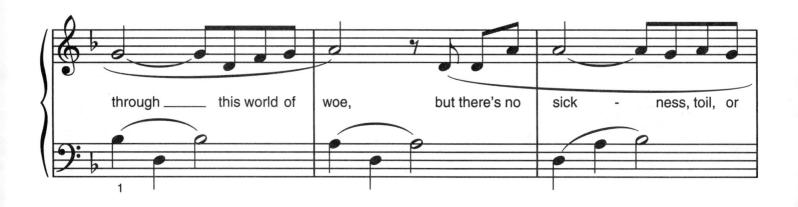

through _____ this world of woe, but there's no sick - ness, toil, or

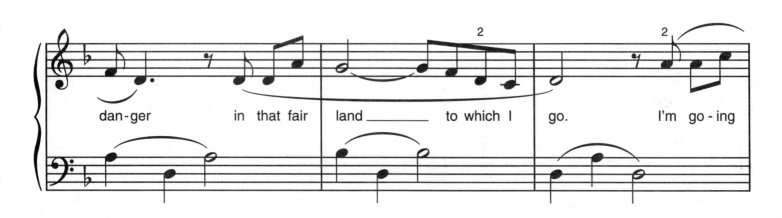

dan-ger in that fair land _____ to which I go. I'm go-ing

Wayfaring Stranger - 2 - 1

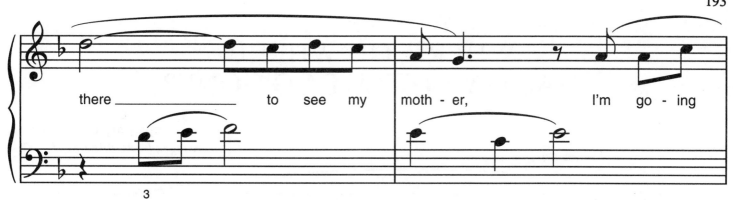

there _____ to see my moth - er, I'm go - ing

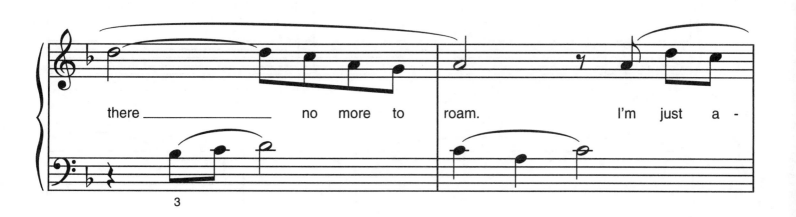

there _____ no more to roam. I'm just a -

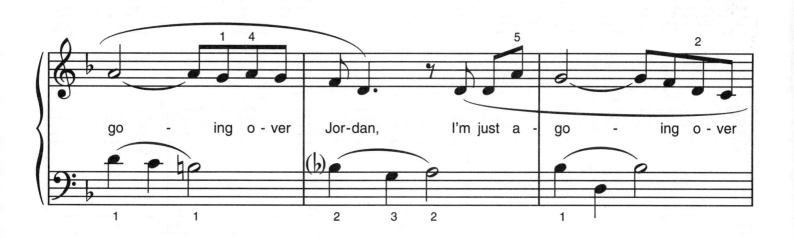

go - ing o - ver Jor-dan, I'm just a - go - ing o - ver

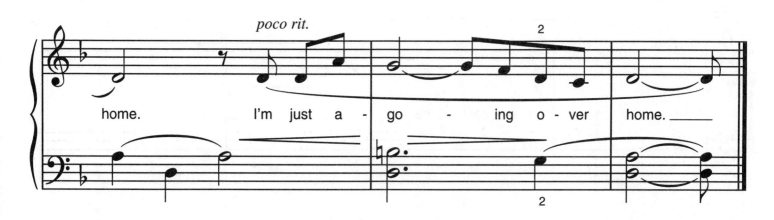

home. I'm just a - go - ing o - ver home. _____

*poco rit.*

# WHERE, OH WHERE
# HAS MY LITTLE DOG GONE?

TRADITIONAL
*Arranged by ROBERT SCHULTZ*

# YANKEE DOODLE

TRADITIONAL
*Arranged by ROBERT SCHULTZ*

*From the Broadway Musical "AIN'T MISBEHAVIN' "*

# AIN'T MISBEHAVIN'

Lyric by
ANDY RAZAF

Music by
THOMAS WALLER and HARRY BROOKS
*Arranged by ROBERT SCHULTZ*

Ain't Misbehavin' - 2 - 1
AS006

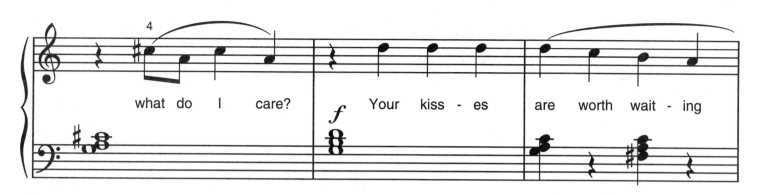

what do I care? Your kiss - es are worth wait - ing

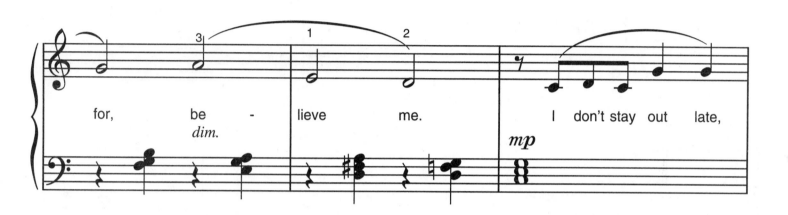

for, be - lieve me. I don't stay out late,

don't care to go, I'm home a - bout eight, just me and my ra - di - o;

ain't mis-be-hav - in', sav-in' my love for you.

*From the Warner Bros. Motion Picture "CASABLANCA"*

# AS TIME GOES BY

Words and Music by
HERMAN HUPFELD
*Arranged by ROBERT SCHULTZ*

# BEI MIR BIST DU SCHON
## (Means That You're Grand)

Original Lyrics by JACOB JACOBS
English Version by
SAMMY CAHN and SAUL CHAPLIN

Music by
SHOLOM SECUNDA
*Arranged by ROBERT SCHULTZ*

*From the Musical Comedy "SWEET CHARITY"*

# BIG SPENDER

Music by
CY COLEMAN

Lyric by
DOROTHY FIELDS
*Arranged by ROBERT SCHULTZ*

*Featured in the Film ''HOLLYWOOD HOTEL'' (Warners 1937)*

# BLUE MOON

Lyric by
LORENZ HART

Music by
RICHARD RODGERS
*Arranged by ROBERT SCHULTZ*

Blue moon, _____ you saw me stand-ing a - lone, _____

_ with-out a dream in my heart, _____ with-out a love of my own. _____

_ Blue moon, _____ you knew just what I was there for, _____

_ you heard me say-ing a prayer for _____ some-one I real-ly could care for. _____

Blue Moon - 2 - 1
AS006

# THE ENTERTAINER

By SCOTT JOPLIN
*Arranged by ROBERT SCHULTZ*

**Easy ragtime tempo**

*From the Motion Picture "MEET ME IN ST. LOUIS"*
# THE TROLLEY SONG

Words by
HUGH MARTIN

Music by
RALPH BLANE
*Arranged by ROBERT SCHULTZ*

**Bright and lively**

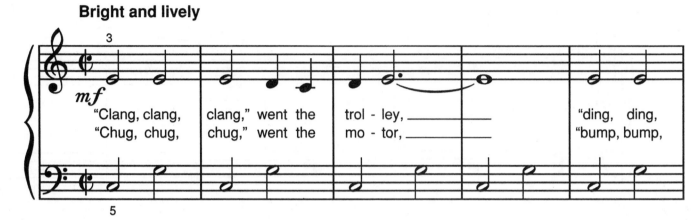

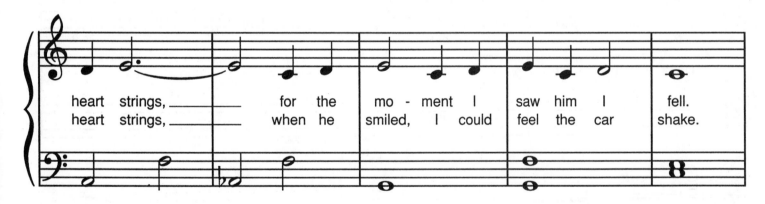

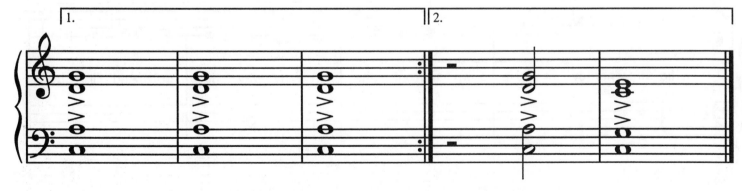

AS006

*From the Broadway Musical "WILDCAT"*

# HEY, LOOK ME OVER

Music by
CY COLEMAN

Lyrics by
CAROLYN LEIGH
*Arranged by ROBERT SCHULTZ*

**Bright march**

*Introduced by LESLIE CARON and MEL FERRER IN "LILI" (MGM 1953)*

# HI-LILI, HI-LO

Words by
HELEN DEUTSCH

Music by
BRONISLAU KAPER
*Arranged by ROBERT SCHULTZ*

Hi-Lili, Hi-Lo - 2 - 1
AS006

# MY WAY

Original French Words by
GILES THIBAULT

English Words by PAUL ANKA
Music by JACQUES REVAUX
and CLAUDE FRANCOIS
*Arranged by ROBERT SCHULTZ*

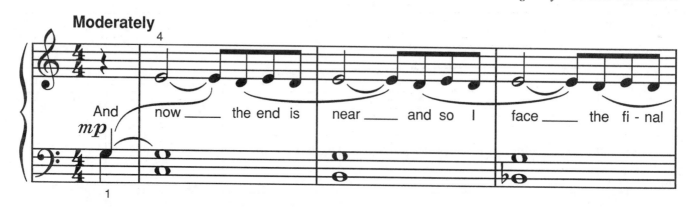

And now ____ the end is near ____ and so I face ____ the fi - nal

cur - tain; my friend, ____ I'll say it clear, ____ I'll state my case, ____ of which I'm

cer - tain. I've lived ____ a life that's full, ____ I've trav-eled each ____ and ev - ery

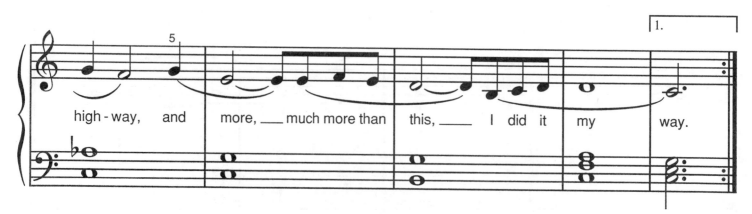

high - way, and more, ____ much more than this, ____ I did it my way.

My Way - 2 - 1
AS006

*Verse 2:*
Regrets, I've had a few, but then again, too few to mention;
I did what I had to do and saw it through without exemption.
I planned each chartered course, each careful step along the byway,
And more, much more than this, I did it my way.

*From the Motion Picture "NEVER ON SUNDAY"*

# NEVER ON SUNDAY

Lyrics by
BILLY TOWNE

Music by
MANOS HADJIDAKIS
*Arranged by ROBERT SCHULTZ*

216

Never on Sunday - 4 - 3

gray day, a May day, a pay day and see if I re - fuse.

And if you make it on a bleak day, a freak day, a

week day, why you can be my guest. But nev - er, nev - er on a

Sun - day, a Sun - day the one day I need a lit - tle rest! *f*

Never on Sunday - 4 - 4

*From the Metro-Goldwyn-Mayer Musical Production "SINGIN' IN THE RAIN"*

# SINGIN' IN THE RAIN

Lyric by
**ARTHUR FREED**

Music by
**NACIO HERB BROWN**
*Arranged by ROBERT SCHULTZ*

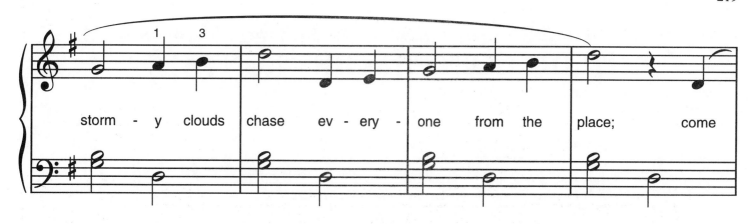

storm - y clouds chase ev - ery - one from the place; come

on with the rain, I've a smile on my face. I'll

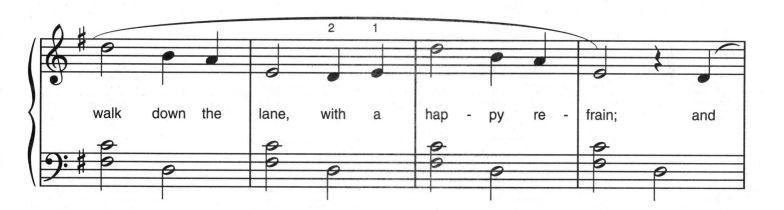

walk down the lane, with a hap - py re - frain; and

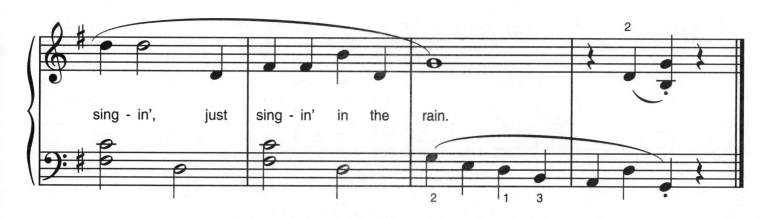

sing - in', just sing - in' in the rain.

*Theme Melody from the 20th Century-Fox CinemaScope Production "THREE COINS IN THE FOUNTAIN"*

# THREE COINS IN THE FOUNTAIN

Words by
SAMMY CAHN

Music by
JULE STYNE
*Arranged by ROBERT SCHULTZ*

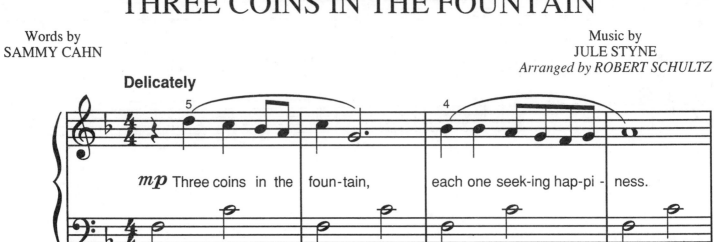

mp Three coins in the foun-tain, each one seek-ing hap-pi - ness.

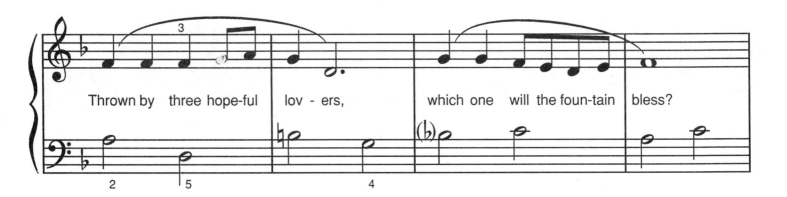

Thrown by three hope-ful lov - ers, which one will the foun-tain bless?

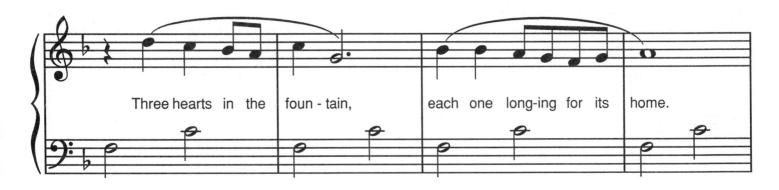

Three hearts in the foun - tain, each one long-ing for its home.

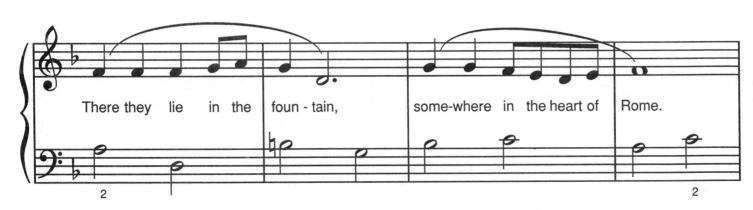

There they lie in the foun - tain, some-where in the heart of Rome.

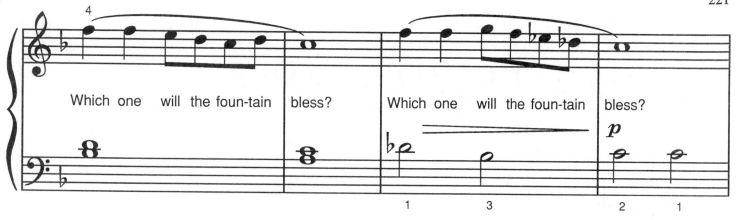

Which one will the foun-tain bless? Which one will the foun-tain bless?
p
mp Three coins in the foun - tain, through the rip-ples how they shine.
Just one wish will be grant - ed, one heart will wear a val - en -
tine. Make it mine! Make it mine! Make it mine!
mf
poco rit.

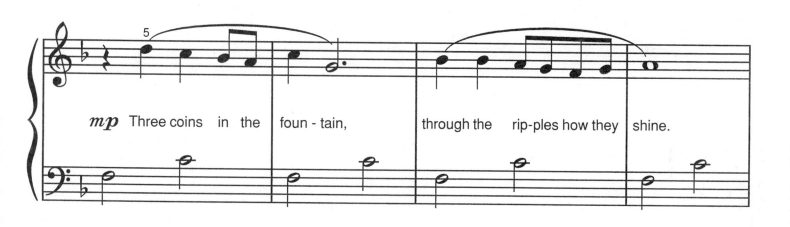

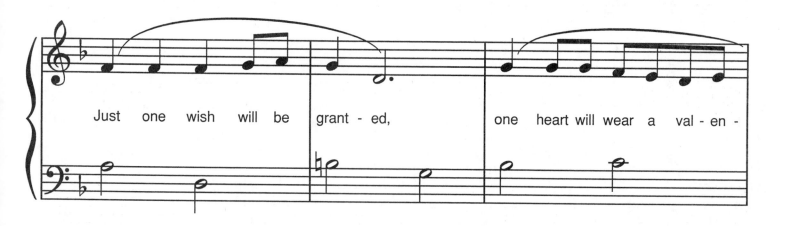

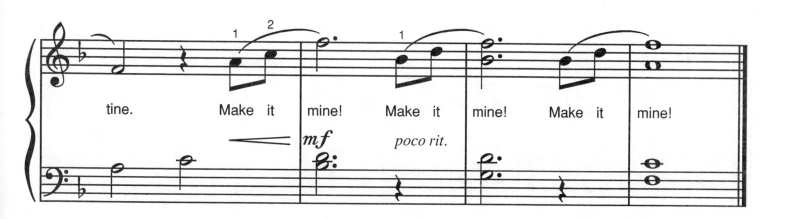

Theme from
# THE ANVIL CHORUS
(from the opera *Il Trovatore*)

GIUSEPPE VERDI
*Arranged by ROBERT SCHULTZ*

**Moderato**

# CRADLE SONG
## (Wiegenlied)

JOHANNES BRAHMS
*Arranged by ROBERT SCHULTZ*

*pedal simile*

Theme from
# BARCAROLLE
(from the opera *The Tales of Hoffmann*)

JACQUES OFFENBACH
*Arranged by ROBERT SCHULTZ*

**Andantino**

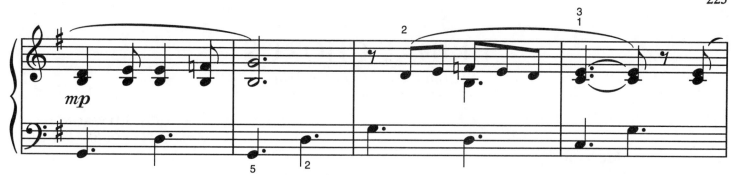

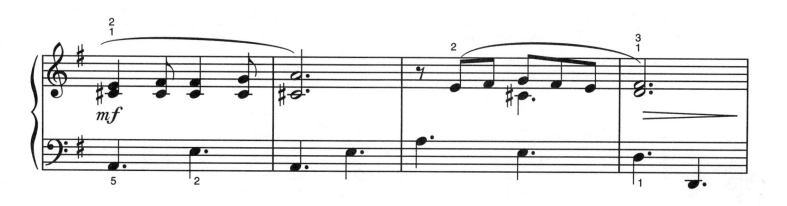

poco rit.

Theme from Barcarolle - 2 - 2

# BRIDAL CHORUS

(from the opera *Lohengrin*)

RICHARD WAGNER
*Arranged by ROBERT SCHULTZ*

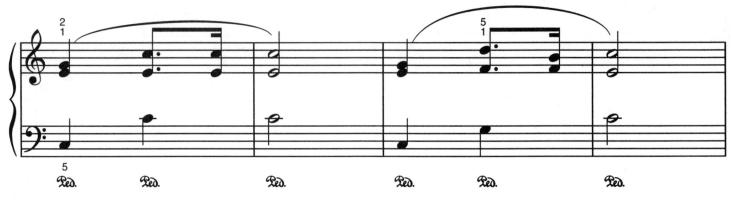

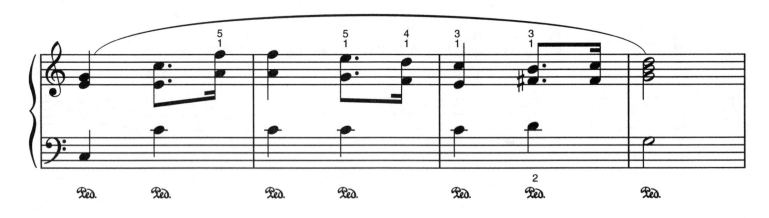

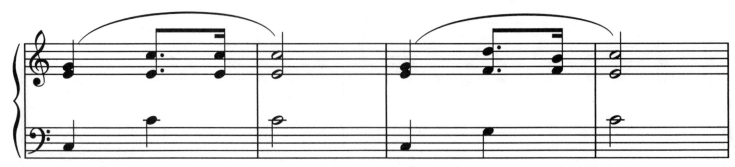

*pedal simile*

Bridal Chorus - 2 - 1

# Theme from
# CAN-CAN
## (from the operetta *La Vie Parisienne*)

JACQUES OFFENBACH
*Arranged by ROBERT SCHULTZ*

**Allegro con brio**

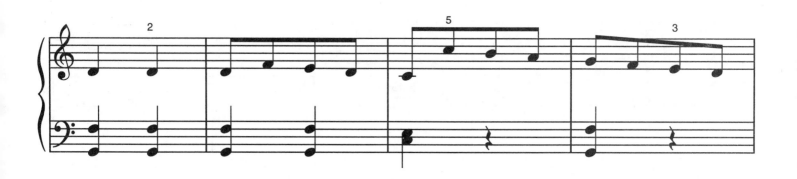

*Fine*

Theme from Can-Can - 2 - 1

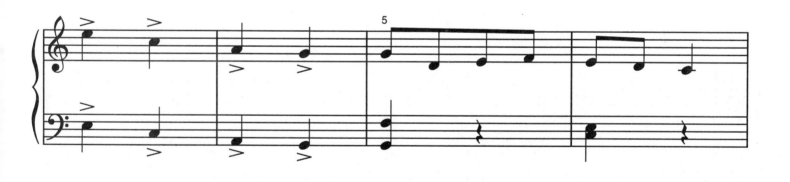

*D.C. al Fine*

Theme from Can-Can - 2 - 2

# Theme from
# CANON IN D

JOHANN PACHELBEL
*Arranged by ROBERT SCHULTZ*

Theme from Canon in D - 2 - 1

Theme from Canon in D - 2 - 2

Theme from
# CHE FARÒ SENZA EURIDICE?
(from the opera *Orfeo ed Euridice*)

CHRISTOPH WILLIBALD GLÜCK
*Arranged by ROBERT SCHULTZ*

# FUNERAL MARCH OF THE MARIONETTES

(from the opera *Faust*)

CHARLES GOUNOD
*Arranged by ROBERT SCHULTZ*

**Misterioso**

# Theme from
# HORNPIPE
(from the D Major Suite from *Water Music*)

GEORGE FREDERIC HANDEL
*Arranged by ROBERT SCHULTZ*

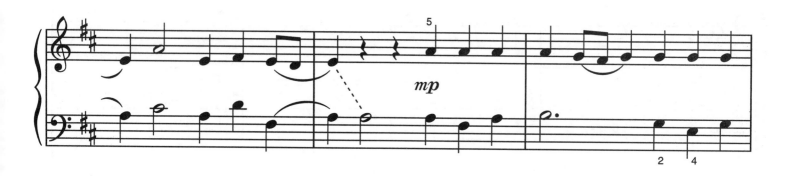

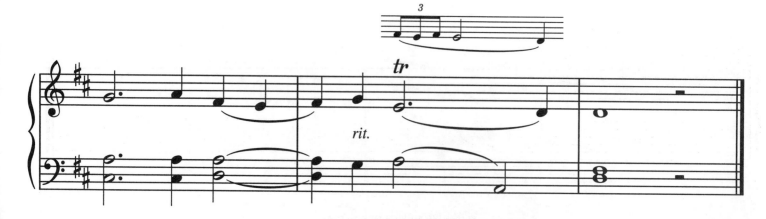

## Theme from
# INTERMEZZO
(from the opera *Cavalleria Rusticana*)

PIETRO MASCAGNI
*Arranged by ROBERT SCHULTZ*

Theme from
# JESU, JOY OF MAN'S DESIRING
(from *Cantata No. 147*)

JOHANN SEBASTIAN BACH
*Arranged by ROBERT SCHULTZ*

Theme from Jesu, Joy of Man's Desiring - 2 - 1

# Theme from
# KOL NIDREI

MAX BRUCH
Op. 47
*Arranged by ROBERT SCHULTZ*

Theme from Kol Nidrei - 2 - 1

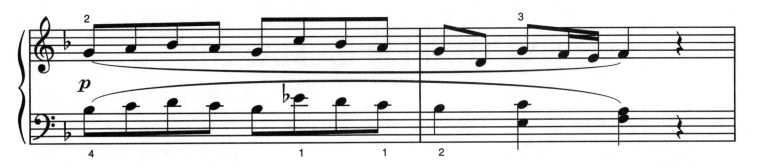

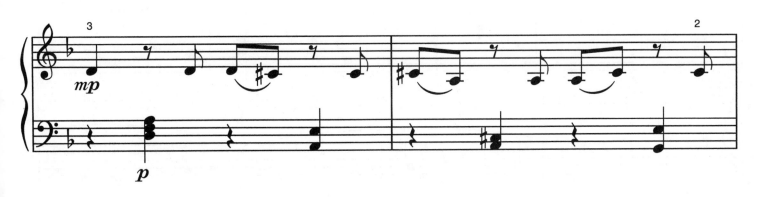

Theme from Kol Nidrei - 2 - 2

Theme from
# LA CI DAREM LA MANO
(from the opera *Don Giovanni*)

WOLFGANG AMADEUS MOZART
*Arranged by ROBERT SCHULTZ*

Theme from
# LA MAMMA MORTA
(from the opera *Andrea Chénier*)

UMBERTO GIORDANO
*Arranged by ROBERT SCHULTZ*

# Theme from
# LARGO
### (from *The New World Symphony*)

ANTONÍN DVOŘÁK
*Arranged by ROBERT SCHULTZ*

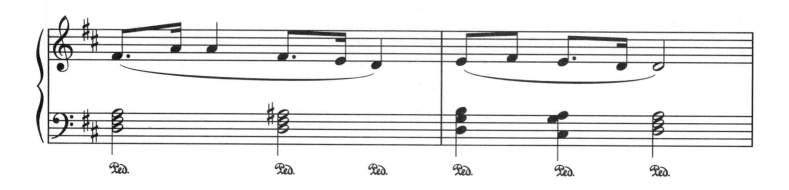

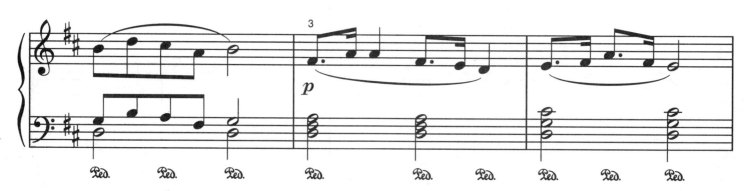

Theme from Largo - 2 - 1

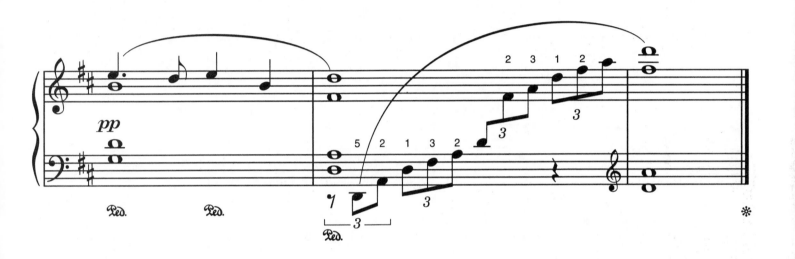

Theme from Largo - 2 - 2

Theme from
# THE MERRY WIDOW
(Waltz)

FRANZ LEHAR
*Arranged by ROBERT SCHULTZ*

Theme from The Merry Widow - 2 - 1

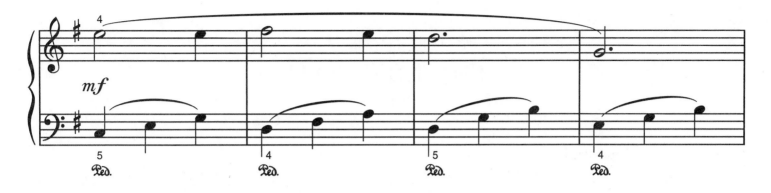

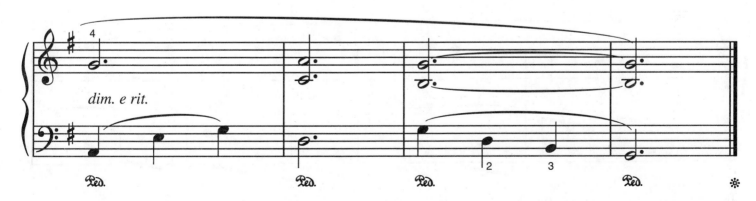

Theme from The Merry Widow - 2 - 2

Theme from
# THE MOLDAU
(Vltava)
(from the Symphonic Poem Cycle *My Country*)

BEDŘICH SMETANA
*Arranged by ROBERT SCHULTZ*

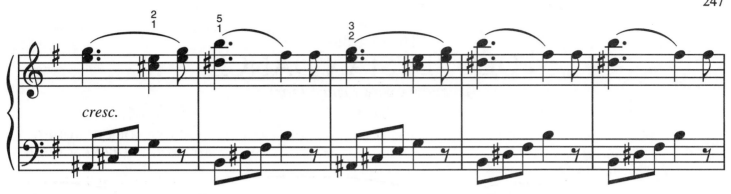

The Moldau - 2 - 2

# Theme from
# POLOVETSIAN DANCE
(from the opera *Prince Igor*)

ALEXANDER BORODIN
*Arranged by ROBERT SCHULTZ*

# RONDEAU THEME
(from *Symphonic Suite No. 1*)

JEAN JOSEPH MOURET
*Arranged by ROBERT SCHULTZ*

# Theme from
# SLAVONIC DANCE

ANTONÍN DVOŘÁK
Op. 46, No. 7
*Arranged by ROBERT SCHULTZ*

**Allegro**

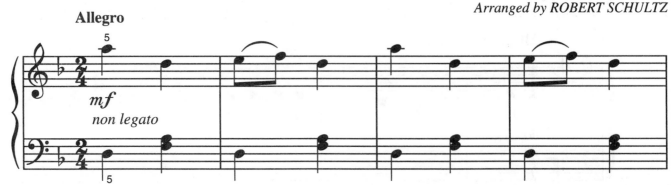

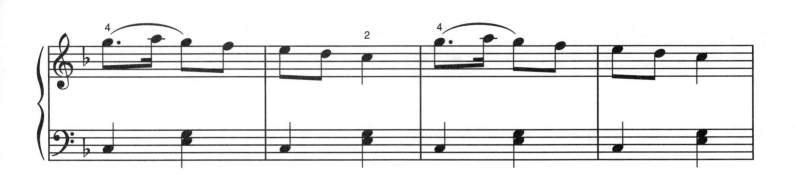

Theme from Slavonic Dance - 2 - 1

Theme from Slavonic Dance - 2 - 2

# Theme from
# THE SORCERER'S APPRENTICE

PAUL DUKAS
*Arranged by ROBERT SCHULTZ*

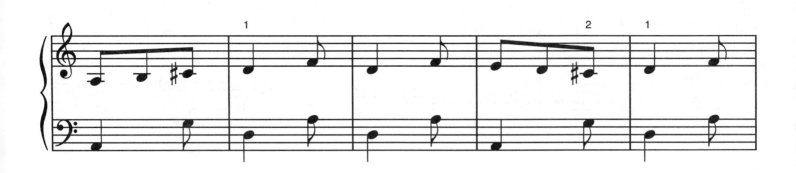

Theme from The Sorcerer's Apprentice - 2 - 2

# Theme from
# SYMPHONY No. 5

LUDWIG VAN BEETHOVEN
*Arranged by ROBERT SCHULTZ*

**Allegro con brio**

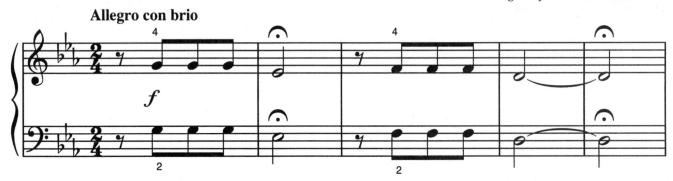

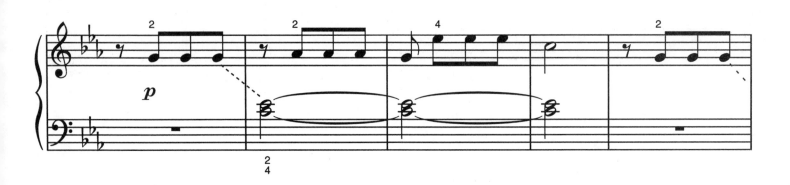

Theme from Symphony No. 5 - 2 - 1

Theme from Symphony No. 5 - 2 - 2

Theme from
# SYMPHONY No. 5
(Movement I)

PETER ILYICH TCHAIKOVSKY
Op. 64
*Arranged by ROBERT SCHULTZ*

**Andante**

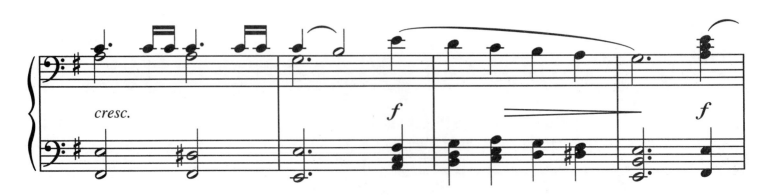

Symphony No. 5 - 2 - 1

Symphony No. 5 - 2 - 2

# Theme from
# SYMPHONY No. 5
## (Movement III - *Waltz*)

PETER ILYICH TCHAIKOVSKY
Op. 64
*Arranged by ROBERT SCHULTZ*

**Allegro moderato**

# Theme from
# SYMPHONY No. 9
### (*Choral Symphony*)

LUDWIG VAN BEETHOVEN
*Arranged by ROBERT SCHULTZ*

Theme from
# SYMPHONY No. 8
*(Unfinished)*

FRANZ SCHUBERT
*Arranged by ROBERT SCHULTZ*

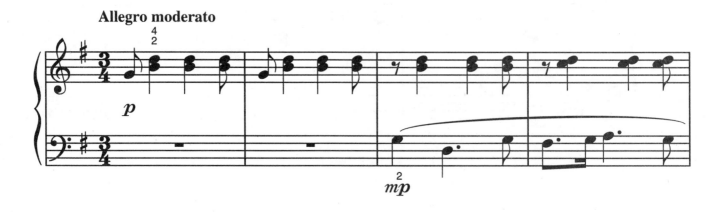

Symphony No. 8 - 2 - 1

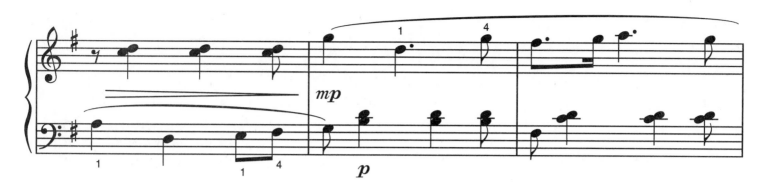

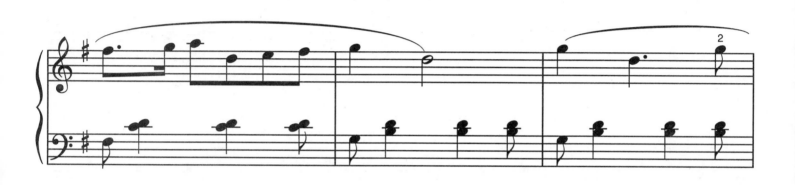

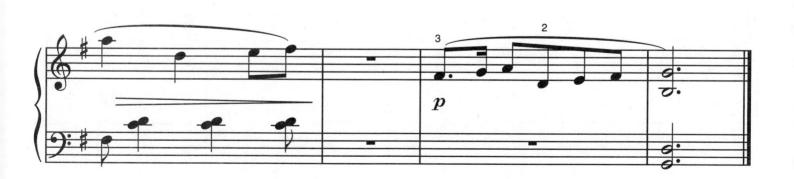

Symphony No. 8 - 2 - 2

# Theme from
# SYMPHONY No. 94
(*Surprise Symphony*)

FRANZ JOSEPH HAYDN
*Arranged by ROBERT SCHULTZ*

Theme from Symphony No. 94 - 2 - 1

Theme from Symphony No. 94 - 2 - 2

# TOYLAND

### (from the operetta *Babes In Toyland*)

Words by
GLEN MacDONOUGH

Music by
VICTOR HERBERT
*Arranged by ROBERT SCHULTZ*

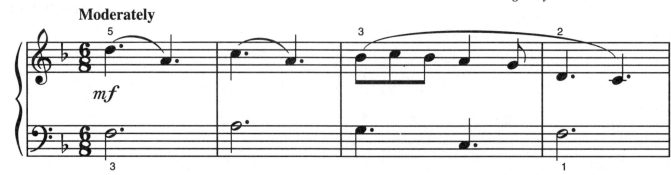

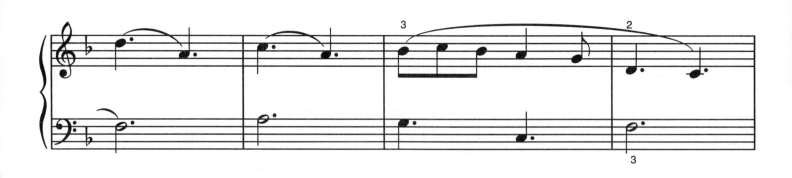

Theme from

# UN BEL DI

(from the opera *Madama Butterfly*)

GIACOMO PUCCINI
*Arranged by ROBERT SCHULTZ*

# WALTZ OF THE FLOWERS
## (from *The Nutcracker Suite*)

PETER ILYICH TCHAIKOVSKY
*Arranged by ROBERT SCHULTZ*

Waltz of the Flowers - 4 - 1

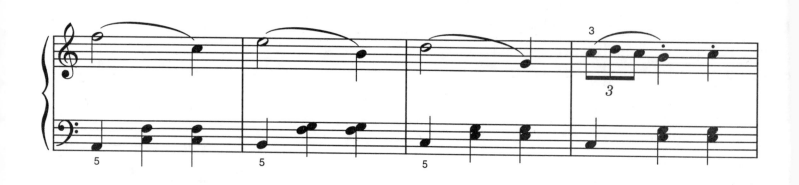

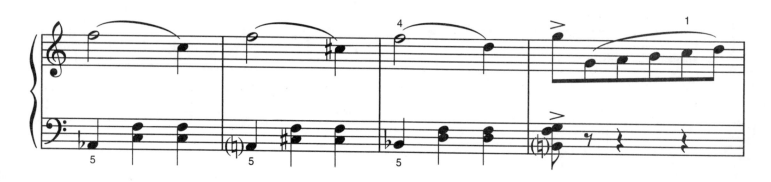

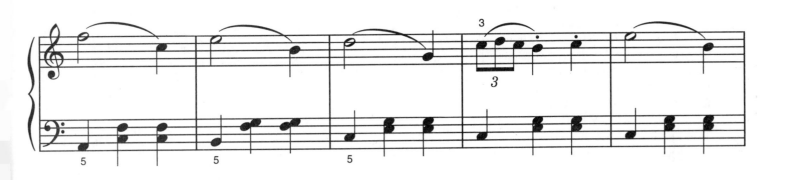

Waltz of the Flowers - 4 - 4

# ALPHABETICAL INDEX

# CLASSICAL MUSIC COLLECTIONS
## from the Schultz Piano Library
### *by Robert Schultz*

Superb editions of the world's best-loved classical music
for piano students at every level from beginner to late intermediate.

## Classical Collections for beginning piano students:

An introduction to classical music through 5-finger arrangements of
well-known themes and beautiful melodies from operas, symphonies,
ballets, chamber music and vocal works.

**Classical Piano Solos for Kids** (AF9823)
45 pieces, 64 pages, Preface, Composer List - names/dates/period.

**Fun with 5 Finger Classical Themes** (AF9765)
35 pieces, 48 pages, Preface.

**Performance Plus® Series — Classical Themes, Book 1** (AF9638)
10 pieces with teacher accompaniments, 24 pages.

## Classical Collections for early to late intermediate piano students:

**Classical Piano Solos for Young Adults** (AF9551)
Early intermediate — 10 easy pieces in their original form by various composers, plus 20 arrangements of well-known themes from the symphony
and opera; 48 pages, Preface.

**Performance Plus® Series — Classical Themes, Book 2** (AF9644)
Early intermediate — 11 arrangements with teacher accompaniments
of themes from symphonies and the opera; 24 pages.

**100 Best Loved Piano Solos — Teaching Pieces** (AF9603)
Early intermediate — 75 easy piano solos in their original form by
composers from all periods, plus 25 arrangements of opera, symphony, vocal and chamber music themes; 156 pages.

**100 Best Loved Piano Solos — Composer Pieces** (AF9503A)
Late intermediate — 90 piano solos in their original form by composers from all periods, plus 10 arrangements of orchestral, vocal and
chamber masterpieces; 256 pages.

**Available at leading music dealers everywhere,
from Warner Bros. Publications**

AD 369  8/99